Lies That Matter

Other Books by Allan Gerson

The Price of Terror: The History-Making Struggle for Justice After Pan Am 103 (with Jerry Adler)

Privatizing Peace: From Conflict to Security (with Nat Coletta)

The Kirkpatrick Mission: Diplomacy Without Apology – America at the United Nations, 1981-1985

Lawyers' Ethics: Contemporary Dilemmas

Israel, the West Bank and International Law

Lies That Matter

A federal prosecutor and child of Holocaust survivors, tasked with stripping US citizenship from aged Nazi collaborators, finds himself caught in the middle

by Allan Gerson

Washington, DC

Copyright © 2021 by The Allan Gerson Estate
New Academia Publishing, 2021

All rights reserved. No part of this book may be reproduced or transmitted in any form or by any means, electronic or mechanical, including photocopying, recording, or by any information storage and retrieval system.

Printed in the United States of America

Library of Congress Control Number: 2021932539
ISBN 978-1-7348659-5-0 paperback
ISBN 978-1-7359378-5-4 hardcover

 An imprint of New Academia Publishing

 4401-A Connecticut Ave., NW #236 - Washington DC 20008
info@newacademia.com - www.newacademia.com

He tried to sing, singing
Not to remember
His true life of lies
And to remember
His lying life of truths

 —*Allan Gerson, April 12, 1987*

If he were alive to write it, I imagine my father would dedicate this book to his mother, Peshka, his father, Mottel, to Raya and Moishe and Ruchsha and the other survivors that brought him to life, to tradition, and to survival against all odds. He would dedicate this book to his brother, children, and grandchildren the branches of his tree, the products of those that lived. He would dedicate this book to my mother, Joan, for supporting him through this complex life he led.

 But I am writing this. Not him. My father passed away on December 1st after battling a brain disease that took him away just as he was putting the finishing touches on this memoir.

 This book is dedicated to my father, Allan Gerson. May you, like I did, inherit his devotion to beauty, complexity, and justice as you read these pages.

 —*Merissa Nathan Gerson, August 20, 2020*

Contents

Foreword by Wolf Blitzer	ix
Acknowledgements	xiii
Introduction: Tormentors, Victims, and the Lies That Enabled Entry into Post-War America	1
Chapter One: A Most Unusual Offer	9
Chapter Two: Zamość: Poland's Urban Gem, My Ancestral Home	23
Chapter Three: Rockler, Rostow, Talleyrand and "Zeal"	31
Chapter Four: Pawns in a Transcontinental Struggle	41
Chapter Five: Rockler's Mind: Mired in the Past	49
Chapter Six: Surviving the War	59
Chapter Seven: Miami Chills	69
Chapter Eight: The Remnant	77
Chapter Nine: A Calculus of Evil	87
Chapter Ten: Never Forget, Never Forgive	107
Chapter Eleven: Leap of Faith	115
Chapter Twelve: True Identity	125
Chapter Thirteen: Trial and Consequences	135
Chapter Fourteen: Civiletti's Argument	153
Chapter Fifteen: Like Actors on a Stage	165
Chapter Sixteen: Fedorenko's Verdict	177
Chapteer Seventeen: Till the Ends of Justice	183
Epilogue: Encountering History	191
Photo Gallery	201
About the Author	223

Foreword by Wolf Blitzer

Allan and I were very good friends for more than 40 years. It was a friendship rooted in a lot of shared history. We both graduated from the State University New York at Buffalo – though we didn't know each other there. He was a few years older. We both loved history, politics and international affairs and that made us news junkies – though we played out that love with very different career paths.

But I suspect what clearly made our friendship so special were our common family roots. Our parents were Polish Jews and Holocaust survivors – wonderful and very courageous people who built new lives in the United States after World War II. His family settled in the Bronx; my family in Buffalo.

We didn't meet until we were both working and living in the Washington, D.C. area. We quickly discovered that we shared a very special bonding experience growing up hearing our parents speak Yiddish and that clearly had an impact. Indeed, over the years, we developed certain Yiddish phrases that found their way into our conversation – and into our laughter.

For example, when our families were having dinner at Joan and Allan's house (and that was often) we would often sit next to each other and when Joan prepared a delicious and very special course we would both take a bite and then look at each other and simply say with a smile:

"Mahne Zoynim Zul Nischt Vissen Fin Ah Zahn Tahm."

Which loosely translated means: "My enemies should never know from such a taste."

By the way, Allan's Yiddish was a lot better than mine. He would often throw out expressions that sounded truly amazing but I'm not even sure they were real Yiddish. I had no idea what he was saying. But they sounded great.

Very often, after that wonderful and delicious meal, we would have a more serious discussion about what's going on in the world and all the serious problems we were facing.

His true passion was justice. That's why he went to work at the U.S. Justice Department in Washington in the Office of Special Investigations. His job was to find Nazi collaborators who had managed to find their way to the United States after the war. They were concentration camp guards, chiefs of auxiliary police and active fascist sympathizers. The Office won rulings against more than 100 Nazi collaborators.

His pursuit of justice also led him to become the senior counsel to the United States delegation to the United Nations Commission on Human Rights.

Had he simply been a graduate of the University at Buffalo, NYU Law School, the Hebrew University of Jerusalem and Yale Law School – and become a legal scholar – that would have been so impressive.

Had he simply been a successful Justice Department trial lawyer pursuing Nazi war criminals – that would have been amazing.

Had he simply been a legal counsel to two U.S. Ambassadors to the United Nations – that would been truly wonderful. (Dayenu!)

Had he simply been a great and innovative lawyer coming up with new ways to sue foreign regimes that kill Americans – that would have been so terrific.

All that is, of course, impressive – but even more important – he was a truly great person, a wonderful friend, a loving father and grandfather and a fabulous husband.

Beyond those impressive achievements, Allan was a very funny guy. He had a great sense of humor but it often came through with some serious context. It must have come from his Bronx/Borscht Belt background.

And often, in the tradition of Yiddish and the Jewish people, we would wind up our serious conversation with these words:

"Ah Bee Gezunt."
"As long as you're healthy."

When I saw Allan during the last few weeks of his life, I would also make a point of saying some Yiddish phrases – and he would of course respond as best as he could with his health clearly deteriorating. It was a source of comfort that our Yiddish brought a little smile to his face. I know his parents and my parents would have been so proud that we tried not to forget their loving language.

In short, Allan Gerson was a very special person.

Read this powerful and revealing memoir – and you will emerge with a real appreciation of his accomplishments and his extraordinary life.

—*Wolf Blitzer, August 2020*

Acknowledgements

This book was Allan's devotion in the last years of his life. The process of writing this book revealed not only layers of his professional work, but also new layers of him to all of those around in the last year of his life.

Allan must have known that his brain was unraveling the summer before he passed on December 1, 2019. He kept saying that he had a real deadline to finish his book, as he sat fixed in front of the manuscript each day on Martha's Vineyard. He was committed to this story's continuity. A story not just of the law, but of his own life, his parents and brothers' lives, and of his connection to other illegal "Dreamers" of today. This was, in essence, a manifesto of the life of Allan Gerson. This would be his final gift to all of us.

We want to thank everyone who supported Allan and our family in the creation of this book, those who listened, reviewed and contributed to piecing this story together, and especially to Anna Lawton who helped us leverage this story to publication. I also want to thank my children, Daniela, David and Merissa, who took on the task of completing this book when their father could not. And, of course, it is our inimitable, sorely missed Allan, who was so much to so many, who we thank for leaving us this personal legacy of his life.

—Joan Nathan Gerson, July 26, 2020

Introduction

Tormentors, Victims, and the Lies that Enabled Entry into Post-War America

In 1979 I became the first trial attorney with OSI, a newly created unit in the Justice Department's Criminal Division. Formally known as the Office of Special Investigations, its task was as formidable as it was laudable: to cleanse the stain on America's honor for failing in the aftermath of the Holocaust to identify Nazi collaborators—concentration camp guards, chiefs of auxiliary police, and active fascist sympathizers—who had succeeded in gaining entry to the U.S. On visa forms they had sworn "NO" to the question of whether they had assisted in the persecution of civilians. Instead, concentration camp guards claimed they had spent the war years as accountants. Chiefs of local auxiliary police, who needed no prompting from the Nazis to do their barbaric work, claimed they had been dairy farmers. No one seemed short on inventiveness.

Had they answered differently, or more tentatively, or descriptively, of their war-time roles, that would have been the end of it—VISA DENIED—or it would have triggered an investigation that would have likely reached the same result. For the lies they projected were paper-thin, thin enough to fail if subjected to proper scrutiny.

To be sure, these men and women bore little resemblance to the masterminds like Herman Goering, Heinrich Himmler and the commandants of the major concentration and extermination camps, those who were put on trial in the grand spectacle of the Nuremberg Proceedings Against Major Nazi War Criminals. Perhaps precisely because of their relatively low-level status, these collaborators, who proved indispensable to the Nazis' heralded Final Solution, of a Europe cleansed of its Jews, often got an easy pass in coming into America.

Having thus made their way into the United States, they went on to acquire US citizenship based on those misrepresentations. For the most part, they went on to lead quiet, uneventful lives as American citizens, respected by their neighbors and contributing to the health and well-being of the communities in which they settled. OSI was established to shatter that facade of normalcy. For what these individuals had done, or stood accused of having done, was far removed from normalcy by any standard. OSI's task was to expose the perpetrators and identify their role, small or large, in the mass roundups and killings referred to as the Holocaust. For the charges against them would detail the ways in which they, as cogs in the gruesome enterprise of industrial genocide, enabled it to occur on a level theretofore unknown to man.

These charges were folded into official Justice Department submissions to the US federal courts, calling upon the courts to denaturalize these individuals, and derivatively their children, thus stripping them of their US citizenship and subjecting them to deportation, usually to their countries of origin.

It was all supposed to function smoothly, like a well-choreographed dance step, and would have, were it not for the circuitous route OSI assumed in going about this task. For OSI's pursuit was driven less by demonstrable proof of the defendant's role in perpetration of mass murder than by establishing convincingly that he or she had lied about it to US consular officials: particularly, that they had committed—in the language of the governing statute—a "material misrepresentation" on their visa application forms. A lie unrelated to the procurement of their visa was thus *immaterial,* of no consequence. Phrased differently, a lie was *material* if, had the truth been disclosed, it would have led to denial of their visa applications. And insofar as their grant of US citizenship was based on those misrepresentations, their US citizenship was tainted, ripe for OSI to ask that it be deemed void, along with all the rights and privileges that pertain to US citizenship.

But despite the fact that the law automatically barred entry into America of those whose applications were marred by material misrepresentations, such misrepresentations were rarely spotted. Indeed, in some special instances, if such follow-up questioning occurred, it would prove to be stymied by orders from above. If their entry was part of Operation Paper Clip, (allowing a specified number of Germany's top rocket scientists, and others with special intelligence information or capabilities, to enter America with no questions asked), top US national security agencies had taken steps to preclude inquiries by OSI and others, declaring individuals associated with that program off-limits for investigation.

That left investigations into collaborators who provided "assistance" relegated to assistance of a lower order. Here an unlikely confluence of interests emerged by the 1970s, which led to OSI's creation and shaped its work. Since the early 1950s, reports had simmered of *the Nazis among us*, but with only sporadic follow-up action by the Justice Department. At the same time, the Soviet Union began to find itself faced with increasingly vocal separatist movements, clamoring for independence. It decided to defang those movements with a two-pronged pincer movement. One pincer would affect decisions within the United States about enforcement of its immigration laws, and thus show the long reach of Soviet justice. For this purpose, it would release files in its possession of individuals deemed Nazi collaborators who had found their way to America. It so happened that most of those who were to be exposed had relatives who remained behind the Iron Curtain, and, not surprisingly, of these many were now active in separatist causes.

In this context, bringing light to bear on the unsavory past of American naturalized citizens of Soviet origin was seen by the Soviets as the way to score a double victory. First, it would affect the immigration status of these individuals through spurring the US Justice Department to institute denaturalization and deportation proceedings against them. This would demonstrate the long reach of Soviet justice, even beyond its reach in exacting retribution against Nazi collaborators. It wouldn't take long for separatists to realize that the Soviets extended far beyond its own borders, with the attendant effect of chilling their ardor.

Thus began, with the aid of various pro-Soviet outlets throughout America, the Soviets' orchestrated release of Nazi collaborator files on American naturalized citizens. Before long, the campaign found its mark. Alarmed Americans began pushing Congress to do something about the thousands of Nazi collaborators reportedly living in America, perhaps next door. Various members of Congress took up their cause. Chief among these was a fiery young congresswoman, Elizabeth Holtzman of New York, who had made a name for herself in the Watergate impeachment proceedings. Under her prodding, working in tandem with the Chairman of the House Judiciary Committee, Peter Rodino, Congress enacted legislation in early 1979 mandating that the Justice Department set up a special unit—OSI—to once and for all deal with the situation. It was to be accorded all the resources it needed in righting America's shame in having been less than scrupulous in ferreting out Nazis and their collaborators in the early post-war years.

It didn't take long, however, to realize that the task before OSI would be far more complicated than imagined. Taking away US citizenship is no matter to be taken lightly. And here the complications were enormous. Take, for example, OSI's mandate to bring proceedings against individuals who were barred from entry by virtue of having "assisted in the persecution of civilians." To get around that prohibition, many who clamored for entry into America had to resort to fraud, misrepresenting the nature of their work during the war years. And to set the record straight would require careful examination and collection of original documents from the *Wehrmacht* and German SS personnel files. These were now predominantly in the possession of the Soviet Union, which had gained control of the German documents. The trouble was that the Cold War was in progress and suspicions ran high as to whether documents were original and untampered-with, and whether they were provided on a selective basis to discredit those with ties to separatist or human rights groups.

But competing with American human rights concerns about such unsavory cooperation was a countervailing tendency that gripped the country and made strict enforcement of US immigration laws the order of the day. And no single group in America at the time seemed more unpopular and deserving of expulsion than the Nazi collaborators who had settled on our shores—concentration camp guards, chiefs of auxiliary police, heads of fascist movements—all of whom had lied their way into America, past its less-than-diligent cadre of US consular officers.

Questions quickly surfaced in my mind that left me agitated and uncertain as to whether we were fitting the punishment to the crime. If the charged offense was merely misrepresentations on visa forms, rather than crimes of the most despicable kind, denial to the defendants of same due process rights accorded to the accused in any court in America seemed inappropriate.

But, to be sure, few had trouble recognizing that the underlying charge, even if not articulated, was that of accessory to mass murder; to genocide. So later, in 1981, when the US Supreme Court, in *US v. Federenko,* upheld the deportation of the defendant directly to the USSR, where we had reason to know a firing squad would await conclusion of a dummy trial, it aroused no concern that a charge of misrepresentation would lead to treatment as a capital offense.

Misrepresentation in visa and citizenship applications is a matter of US immigration law, and few if any of the normal due process rights accorded to defendants in criminal trials apply. Although OSI was housed in the Criminal Division and reported to its ranking assistant attorney general, US immigration law, not criminal law, governed its proceedings. The mirage that sustained this non-application of criminal law is that OSI was not dealing with *punitive* remedies, which are the realm of the criminal justice system, but merely with visa- and citizenship-related misrepresentations, which are in the realm of the immigration legal system. And so deportations to the USSR followed by a firing squad were seen as not really "punitive," as if lives were not at stake.

Who were they, the individuals who fell into this anomalous category of "misrepresenters" deserving of being sent back to likely death? Most were former Ukrainian nationals. Few were rabid haters, anti-Semites to the bone. Primarily, they were men and women who saw in collaboration the means for their just reward at war's end—the lifting of the oppressive Soviet yoke squelching their nation's desire for independence. Others who were the focus of OSI's sights were merely the unlucky ones—conscripts into the Red Army who had the misfortune of being captured early on and then interned in prisoner of war camps where starvation was the order of the day, unless they accepted the Germans' offer of employment as armed concentration camp guards. Opting for collaboration, they, like their political compatriots, became the indispensable cogs of the Nazis' monstrous Final Solution.

On an emotional level this would create difficulties of several orders. My parents were, after all, Holocaust survivors for whom *NEVER FORGET, NEVER FORGIVE* was a code to live by. But they were also immigrants who had to contend with their share of shaving the truth if entry into America was to be assured. And so for me, as for them, retribution took on a different meaning. Deportation could not be the end goal; rather, it would be the establishment of an unassailable record of willing collaboration in enabling the Holocaust. For what example would be set, they asked, if in the end the history books recorded that we were punishing the unwilling collaborators who, like the Jews in the camps who served as *kapos*, had not been acting out of free will?

Something else would set me apart from my fellow prosecutors. I had family secrets. Slowly they would come to the fore, demonstrating that my parents, too, were not beyond the lure of the lie that didn't really seem to matter, but which would suffice nevertheless to get them past the barriers that confounded their entry into the United States.

I had come to believe that my hesitation in telling them about my decision to join OSI was as inexplicable as it was weird. When I told them, I expected nothing less than a shower of pride. But there were no grins of satisfaction, no seeing their son as the redeeming angel for their suffering. Instead, there was only agitation, coupled with a barely disguised plea to reconsider my decision.

In large measure this book is the story of the effort to get to the core of their unease. It takes us to the town of Rawa-Ruska in the Ukraine, 15 kilometers away from that of my parents' hometown of Zamość in eastern Poland, on the other side of the Bug River.

There Wolodomyr Osidach presided as the war-time former chief of police of Rawa-Ruska. And my first OSI case, *US v. Wolodomyr Osidach*, concerns the effort to strip him of his US citizenship. The second case I would become involved with, even if indirectly, *US v. Federenko*, would come before the US Supreme Court and hover over everything I did and questioned at OSI.

Both cases intertwined to raise these nagging questions that it is now time to explore:

Is US immigration law an appropriate vehicle for dealing with efforts at historic justice emanating from war crimes of another era in a foreign place?

If so, at what cost to naturalized Americans whose reconstructed lives will be torn asunder without the benefit of minimal due process routinely accorded defendants in criminal trials?

How essential is proving "free will" to the charge of complicity in the Nazi scourge? In the language of the governing law, "assistance" in persecution is the catchword. But how is it to be defined in trying circumstances? What if it involves those members of the Jewish remnant who served as *kapos*, ushering fellow Jews into the gas chambers and exacting beatings to those grabbing forbidden scraps of food?

"The answers to these questions came slowly, and yielded, along the way, a process of self-discovery." Questions of personal identity intersect with those dealing with America's belated efforts to come to grips with the shortcomings of its ill-equipped US immigration law system to deal with the Nazi collaborators we never weeded out.

In these circumstances, I found myself trying to square my allegiance to accountability with the US government's commitment to strictest enforcement of immigration law across the board. A chasm would develop that would prove difficult to bridge.

Yet at the heart of all these questions of punishment and deficiencies of the US immigration law system in dealing with questions of historic justice, one nagging question in particular tugs at our shirttails: *Which lies really matter? Which are material misrepresentations, and which may be forgiven, and ultimately forgotten?* Lives hang in the balance.

United States Department of Justice

This is to certify that

ALLAN GERSON

is a

TRIAL ATTORNEY

of the
CRIMINAL DIVISION

Order of:
THE ATTORNEY GENERAL
No. 12218

ASSISTANT ATTORNEY GENERAL
FOR ADMINISTRATION

Allan Gerson's Department of Justice trial attorney credentials.

Chapter One

A Most Unusual Job Offer

May, 1979: For the previous year and a half, I had been with the Civil Division of the US Department of Justice. I never had to talk to jurors, cross-examine witnesses, or find any smoking guns. I only dealt with cases on appeal, representing various US government agencies on a gamut of issues. Typically, I wrote straightforward briefs and then appeared before a three-judge panel to deliver a 15-minute oral argument. Opposing counsel did the same, and each case turned on the minutiae of obscure statutory provisions. The work was steady, the hours predictable. The pay was good, and for many, it was the ideal job at Justice.

But was it meaningful? To be sure, the cases often dealt with the limits and breadth of executive power and that of federal agencies, large and small. These were important issues with serious constitutional and civil liberties overtones. But I can't say there was anything profoundly moving me about the position I espoused. I could, more often than not, as easily have espoused that of the opposing side. Sometimes, arguing the government's position made me squirm. Perhaps the most telling case is the first one I was called upon to argue—*Crawford v. US Civil Service Commission*, 5th Circuit Court of Appeals, New Orleans.

Ms. Crawford, the widow of a lifetime US postal employee had been assured by her husband that upon his death she would be well taken care of, by virtue of having assigned his annuity benefits to her. To show her how much he cared that she not be left at any disadvantage, he informed her of extra precautions he had taken to make sure it would all work out. To wit, he showed her a carbon copy of a letter he had typed and sent to the US Civil Service Commission.

> US Civil Service Commission:
>
> I am in receipt of your inquiry as to whether I want my annuity to continue, upon my death, to my wife. I noticed that the form I was supplied for any changes in administration of the annuity called upon me to check a box specifying my intention. Because the language regarding the choice of box to check was somewhat confusing, this is to indicate that 'YES, I want the annuity to continue on behalf of my wife.' I will be providing her a carbon copy. This should allay any questions about my intentions. My intent is to assure that she not be deprived of any income needed to enable her to live out her remaining years in the dignity she deserves.

But Mr. Crawford's best-laid plans went unexpectedly awry. When, upon his death, Ms. Crawford claimed her annuity, the Commission's response was disheartening. "*Sorry, it seems that your husband checked the wrong box.*" Ms. Crawford, proud that her deceased husband had anticipated such an eventuality, took out the carbon copy. To her astonishment, it was deemed of no value. The US Civil Service Commission offered her this explanation.

> We are very sorry, Ms. Crawford, but the Commission cannot be expected to read unsolicited letters. The form is what counts, and on that form he checked the box specifying that he does not want the annuity to continue upon his death.

She was nonplussed. She had been relying on that annuity as the sole source of her retirement income. Had not the carbon copy made clear her husband's intent?

The Commission could not deny that in the carbon copied letter, he had made clear his intentions. But here, another superseding governmental interest imposed itself: "For federal agencies to be required to read every letter sent to it," the Commission responded, "would place too great a burden on the government and undermine the efficiency of its work."

Shocked, Ms. Crawford hired a lawyer to compel the Commission to order payment of the annuity. The district court wasted no time in issuing its order awarding Ms. Crawford the annuity. However, it offered no explanation or rationale for its decision. It's as if they ruled "she deserves it, and let that be the end of it." The alternative, of legitimizing governmental deprivation of widows' annuities solely because a husband had mistakenly checked the wrong box, and especially here, as his intentions were made clear in an accompanying letter, seemed both cruel and undignified. So much so that it didn't require a learned opinion to make the point.

That might have been the end of it had not the Assistant Attorney General of the Civil Division, Barbara Babcock, weighed in on behalf of the government. In an appeal of the decision she argued that it would set an awful precedent making the federal government responsible for reading each and every one of the thousand or more unsolicited letters that came its way concerning this or that decision. Economically speaking, it would be too onerous a burden.

Perhaps because at the time I was the new man on the block at the Civil Division's appellate staff (which handles such appeals), and everyone else (or nearly so) in the section had distanced themselves from being involved in seeking a reversal of the ruling, the task of overturning it, thus depriving Ms. Crawford of her annuity, was assigned to me. Dutifully, I flew to the Fifth Circuit Court of Appeals sitting in New Orleans, to make the government's argument. I felt compelled, however, to preface my remarks with the following short statement: "Your Honors, I have a confession to make. My sympathies, too, lie with Ms. Crawford. But before we can award her the annuity she claims as rightfully hers, there are legal hurdles she must surmount. Unfortunately, they are insurmountable."

The Court of Appeals was in a dilemma. Much as it wanted to affirm the District Court's ruling, the law was not on Ms. Crawford's side. In a Solomonic moment, it hit upon a solution to satisfy all concerns. What the federal government really wanted was that no precedent be set that required the reading of all incoming mail. Ms. Crawford, had no interest in setting a precedent, but only in receiving her annuity. The government had no objection to this, *sans* an obligation to read incoming mail. This could be squared, the Court of Appeals reasoned, by rendering an unpublished opinion (which is legal, although morally dubious), which would award the annuity to Ms. Crawford, with the caveat that the opinion could not be cited as precedent. Therefore, both sides would be satisfied. What good is a judicial opinion, though, if it cannot be cited as precedent? That seemed to defeat the whole purpose of the rule of law.

Moreover, as I saw it, the ruling was in any event of limited utility. Unpublished opinions are a tool that can be relied upon only rarely, usually when compelled by extraordinary equitable circumstances. Otherwise, the rule of law is turned topsy-turvy, ignoring the dual principles that gird the law and assure respect for its rulings: equal application of the law and transparency. Still, the ruling did have the virtue of making clear that strict adherence to the letter of the law without attention to context is a self-defeating stratagem. For law drained of the spirit in which it was conceived becomes a pale imitation of what was intended, subverting the very purpose of the drafters of the legislation. Moreover, absent curbs on the excessive exercise of governmental power, it risks making the government impervious to the consequences of its actions, as if responsible only to itself, and obligated to no one. Perhaps for this reason, the bulk of my professional life has centered on curbing the invocation of *sovereign immunity* to shield it from accountability for its actions.

On my return to Washington, I continued my labors at the Justice Department. With time came a string of successes, and departmental awards testifying to the fact that I had mastered the metier. Yet I yearned for something beyond the rarefied atmosphere of appellate advocacy. For example, I would sit with my fellow appeals attorneys in the Justice Department dining room with a television screen above running images of a civil war in Mozambique, a coup in Somalia, or a terrorist attack in Israel. I would be riveted. My colleagues would be indifferent. I had left an academic career to learn the hard knocks of "real" law practice, yet bringing international law to bear on the conduct of states continued to run strong in my blood. Soon I was asking myself if I really wanted to do another case on behalf of the Comptroller of the Currency in disputes over the reach of state banking law, or defend the power of the National Mediation Board to issue unappealable rulings in disputes in the air, rail, and sea industries. The list goes on and on. To be sure, each case drew in new facts and unfurled new dramas, each with its own challenges. But I wondered: Where did that take me? Being equally adept at arguing either side of a case, with equal dollops of passion, seemed at odds with the life I envisioned. Not that this made my work any different from that of most of my law school classmates who were, if not in government practice, then in the canyons of Wall Street or homespun firms, their shingles out, pronouncing their willingness to serve whatever client came prepared to pay the price. All fine, for them.

But what to do? My wife, Joan, already had a hard enough time understanding why I had ever left teaching to go to Washington. True, the New England School of Law where I taught Contracts, Commercial Law and Professional Ethics wasn't the toniest of law schools. Yet we lived in Cambridge, Massachusetts and had a wide circle of friends and acquaintances.

One of those was Phil Heymann. We had lived near each other on Concord Avenue. He taught at Harvard, and we shared some mutual friends centered around Judge Benjamin Kaplan, also a neighbor, who had been a beloved professor at Harvard Law for many years before recently being elevated to the Massachusetts Supreme Court. Phil was respected by nearly all as soft-spoken, yet tough, a first-rate scholar who was also politically astute and seemed to have a knack for landing on the right side of history. In 1971, he had joined his Harvard colleagues in writing an open letter to Congress calling for an end to the Vietnam War, and he later assisted both Archibald Cox and Leon Jaworski in their role as Special Counsel to investigate crimes associated with the Watergate scandal. Somehow, whenever we would meet, Phil would take an interest in me, my background, my interest in international affairs, and generally, where I was headed in life. Several months earlier, Phil had been offered the post of assistant attorney general of Justice's Criminal Division, to which OSI reported. He immediately accepted and took a leave of absence from his teaching post.

I told Phil that I was looking for something more exciting. That didn't surprise him. I hardly needed to spell out that I had no significant knowledge of criminal law and lacked trial experience. After graduating NYU Law School in 1969, I had opted for a teaching job in an inner city school (where I became in charge of discipline, drawing on my martial arts/college wrestling experience) to earn a draft deferment during the Vietnam period, and then went on to do a masters at the Hebrew University in Jerusalem and a doctorate at Yale. That in turn led me to a law teaching job in Boston. My stint as an appeals lawyer with the Civil Division followed. But none of this made for sterling credentials for some unidentified position with the Criminal Division.

Phil understood, but was not deterred. He related to me that a new unit was being established at Justice, dubbed OSI for Office of Special Investigations. It would be housed in the Criminal Division even though its work had nothing to do with the application of US criminal law. US immigration law would govern. Nor did it require of its attorneys that they master the intricacies of US criminal law with all its provisions of due process for the defendants. Immigration law was a different kettle of fish. And as for no trial experience, not to worry, these proceedings would be before US district court judges without the presence of any jury. OSI's task, he explained, involved a hot potato that had been roiling Congress in the last few years: calls to do something about the persistent rumors, and mounting evidence, that thousands of Nazi collaborators had infiltrated the United States after the war by disguising their sordid past. Now OSI would take up the cudgel of finding them, stripping them of their US citizenship, and ultimately deporting them to the Soviet Union, which had its own score to settle with them.

This wasn't going to be a rerun, writ small, of the Nuremberg War Crimes Trials that followed in the wake of World War II. No one would be prosecuted for war crimes. OSI's interest was fraud, immigration fraud—*"material misrepresentation,"* in the words of the governing statute—presumably about their wartime role as Nazi collaborators. No banner was required to spell out to those seeking entry, that a word or chirp about their ignoble past would lead to automatic rejection of their quest for a US visa. And now, some thirty years later, the collaborators stood to lose their coveted US citizenship, and then face deportation.

"OSI seems right up your alley," Phil told me, "a cross between criminal and civil law."

I nodded, somewhat hesitantly. To be sure, the idea intrigued me, but I had questions. What were we ultimately trying to achieve?

"Besides," he added, "your parents are Holocaust survivors, aren't they?"

"They are," I replied matter-of-factly. The comment rankled me, as if personal vendettas or thoughts of being an avenging angel had anything to do with a professional assignment.

Phil spotted my unease, and, as if to deflect any quick decision, encouraged me to first get a fuller picture of the job by meeting with Walter Rockler, a former Nuremberg prosecutor who had been named OSI's first director. "You will like Rockler," Phil said. "Go see him."

As soon as I got back to my office in the Civil Division, I quickly dialed the number Phil had given me and got in touch with Rockler's secretary to arrange an appointment at the next available date. It was long before the age of the Internet but it didn't take long for me, in the Main Justice Library, to get the information I needed about OSI. No government bureaucracy simply stumbles into existence, and OSI was no exception. For the past two or three years a movement in the United States to track down and deport Nazi war criminals in America had been building up a head of steam. In part, the movement was spurred by a 1976 best-selling book, *Wanted! The Search for Nazis in America*, and by a four-part miniseries in 1978, titled *Holocaust*, which won four Emmy Awards, including one for Meryl Streep. Then there was the notorious case of Hermine Braunsteiner-Ryan, a housewife in Queens who had immigrated from Austria. When the authorities discovered that she had been a guard at two different concentration camps—allegedly whipping women to death and shoving children into trucks on their way to the gas chambers—her citizenship was revoked, and in 1973 she was extradited to Germany.

The specter of Nazis roaming safely through America, comfortably integrated into the mainstream and now approaching retirement, also captured the attention of politicians. A Democrat who represented parts of the Bronx and Westchester County, she was first elected in 1972. Serving on the House Judiciary Committee, Holtzman quickly drew the national spotlight during the Watergate hearings. She understood the media, and when she discovered that Nazi war criminals had immigrated to the United States, she held press conferences to demand action.

In fact, relatively few Nazis actually had come to the US. Fearing they would not be safe here, most had gone to South America, particularly Brazil, Chile, and Argentina. But their collaborators were less fearful and came to the United States in far greater numbers—perhaps as many as 10,000, according to official estimates—with most coming from the Baltic states and Ukraine.

Congressional hearings investigated the presence of Nazis and their collaborators, leading to legislation that established a special unit within the Immigration and Naturalization Service (INS). That unit then morphed into OSI as a task force at the Department of Justice, housed in the Criminal Division, to identify, denaturalize, and deport any naturalized citizen who had "assisted" in "persecuting" civilians (of course, "exterminating" would have been a more apt description.).

It was a daunting challenge. The atrocities had occurred decades earlier and thousands of miles away. Much of the documentary proof, including records from the death camps, had been destroyed; other evidence was controlled by the Soviet Union, and the Cold War was still going at full tilt. Nonetheless, with the formation of OSI, the United States at last seemed fully committed to bringing Nazi collaborators to justice.

The odd thing was that, until Phil Heymann told me about it, I had not heard about plans to establish the OSI unit, and I was only dimly aware of the efforts at tracking down Nazi collaborators. True, I was busy in those years with competing demands on my attention: first, the long and burdensome effort of completing my doctorate at Yale (which I finally did in 1976) while simultaneously holding on to a new law teaching position, and then making the transition in 1977 to appellate advocacy in Washington with the Justice Department. Then, a few months later, our daughter Daniela was born (our other two children, Merissa and David, would be born in 1982 and 1985).

My parents were indeed Holocaust survivors (a designation they would reluctantly accept, as they had survived the war in labor camps in Siberia and would always remark that their fate hardly compared to that of those who had survived the extermination camps). And yet, the fate of the surviving Nazis or their collaborators generated little interest to me at that time in my life. Thus, when Phil noted that I was a son of survivors, I bristled at the thought that this fact had anything to do with my qualifications for this job or motives for taking it. Any thoughts of retribution or fantasies of avenging their suffering, which admittedly occupied my imagination during my teenage years, had long since dissipated. What was left was this: an abiding interest in international law and securing accountability for gross human rights abuses. What OSI's mission elicited in me was an undeniable air of intrigue and excitement.

Having done my homework about the impetus for OSI, I sought

to piece together what I could about Walter Rockler. I already knew that Rockler wasn't really a part of DOJ but was a tax attorney at the prestigious Washington law firm of Arnold & Porter (Abe Fortas, an original name partner, had been elevated by President Johnson to the US Supreme Court before being done in by an illicit funds scandal). Because of Rockler's experience at Nuremberg, Phil Heymann had asked him to lead the search for the first director. The fledgling OSI would need someone who could give it instant credibility. Rockler reached out to two major prosecutors at Nuremberg: Telford Taylor, the chief prosecutor; and a deputy, Charles La Follette, but they declined. And so, Phil asked Rockler to take the job.

Rockler also initially declined, saying that he had prosecuted German bankers at Nuremberg and that seemed removed from the work OSI was being called upon to do. However, he eventually realized the similarity and recognized that what he had done after the Second World War and what OSI was now trying to do were different pages from the same book: seeking justice against those who had assisted in the annihilation of Europe's Jews and other so-called "undesirables." Rockler accepted the position on an interim basis: no more than a year, just until the office got up and running. His annual government salary was one dollar.

On May 18, 1979, I was escorted into Rockler's imposing corner suite in the Arnold and Porter office building around the corner from its grand townhouse on 19th Street. Rockler was sitting slumped behind his desk when I walked in. He stood up slowly, as if racked by arthritis, to extend his great big maw of a hand. The handshake was a full-court press, memorable not so much for its strength as for its grasp, with the fleshy area between his thumb and forefinger cutting deeply into that space on my hand.

Now that he was no longer slumped over, I could see that he had a rather large frame. He was balding, and his face was overpowered by thick black-rimmed glasses of the kind more popular a decade earlier. In his shirt pocket was a soft pack of cigarettes. As I was soon to learn, they were always unfiltered Camels, three packs a day, and undoubtedly responsible for the sound of his voice, raspy as grindstone.

Rockler motioned for me to sit in a straight-backed chair facing him at the other side of the desk.

"I see Heymann thinks highly of you. I don't know why. Far as I can make out, you never really practiced law. I'm not knocking it. I see you have plenty of appellate experience, but this job is going to call on interrogation skills and being adept in a courtroom. Don't get me wrong. I'm not saying you're unqualified. I'm just thinking about what Phil had in mind."

His comments threw me off-guard. I had done my homework, so I knew exactly what kind of an interrogator Rockler had been.

Fresh out of Harvard in 1943, he had joined the US Marines, and was, after Japanese language training school, commissioned a second lieutenant and sent packing to the Pacific theater where the most awful fighting of the war was at full tilt. He landed directly with the combat troops, but because he was in intelligence, not infantry, he was able to escape the hail of bullets. He did, however, end up landing on as many islands (if not more) on the seaward march to the Japanese mainland as all but a handful of other living Americans. That he was an intelligence officer interrogating Japanese prisoners in a no-holds-barred war only added to his mystique. The Army Field Manual provided little guidance as to what one could do to garner critical information. Few Japanese soldiers had survived the brutal island cave-by-cave combat. And after being routed by flame-throwers from the tunnels and caves where they had sought shelter, many raced out with a sword in hand, preferring death by *hara-kiri* to capture. These were the hardened men Rockler had to interrogate.

When Japan surrendered on August 15, 1945, Rockler's tour of duty in the Pacific had essentially come to an end. He then returned to complete his final year at Harvard Law School. On graduation there was much talk of America's establishment of a grand tribunal at Nuremberg where the major Allied Powers could put the defendants for trial for crimes against humanity and genocide, both new offenses in international law. Rockler didn't have to think twice. He signed up for service as a prosecutor at the last of the Nuremberg war crimes trials: those against the industrialists and bankers who helped enable and bankroll the Nazis' hideous Final Solution. I told him I knew about all of this.

"I think you'll do just fine," Rockler said abruptly. The interview was over. He offered me the job as OSI's first trial attorney.

"Your badge will say 'Number Three,' after me and the deputy director, who I am still looking for," he said. Rockler let me know that although I wasn't the type of litigator he'd had in mind for the job, what carried the day was that Phil Heymann thought highly of me and that I seemed to be a quick study.

He pulled out a Camel from the soft pack in the breast pocket of his shirt and lit it with an old scratched lighter—World War II vintage. As I recalled from war movies and graphic war-action comic books I had been drawn to as a kid, his lighter had the same unique *klik-klak* sound the comic books had memorialized.

"Look, Allan," he said, "I think it's an important job. But it is for you to decide. If you're really interested, come back and see me in a few days, and we can figure out the rest."

He gave me a wink—the way I guess they did back then—and showed me out the door.

I walked back to my office at Main Justice, heading down Connecticut Avenue to Lafayette Park and across to Pennsylvania Avenue, past the White House entrance. There was no shortage of things to think about. This was reassuringly clear: Rockler seemed at ease with my qualifications for the job despite the fact that I had never prosecuted anyone. He knew I wasn't cast in the mold of criminal prosecutors and he would be looking to others who were, to fill the other trial lawyer positions. There was no mistaking that my outlook differed from theirs, less attuned to the black or white of innocence or guilt, yet mindful of endless shades of gray. But he might well have realized that I had mastered another art, one essential to effective appellate advocacy: a capacity to quickly get to the heart of an issue. I suspected as well that he thought I could bring to the assignment an extra measure of passion from family history, something that Heymann must have shared with him. And in my international law studies, I was already well-acquainted with the Nuremberg proceedings. In any case, the ball was now in my court: Was I really prepared to take on this assignment? I would need to consult with others, beginning with Joan.

Joan might have thought she was going to be an international law professor's wife, but then I gave up pursuing an academic career. She would have been happy if we had stayed in Boston, instead of turning my sights to Washington, D.C., and the bureaucratic life of an appellate advocate with the Justice Department's Civil Division. Joining OSI would be yet another transition. I knew that Joan couldn't help but wonder where my involvement in investigations and deportations of suspected Nazi collaborators could possibly lead, but when I told her I was considering taking the OSI job, she told me, "Follow your heart."

The decision was mine alone to make. Perhaps the die was cast from the moment I shook hands with Rockler and looked him in the eye. We would be co-adventurers in a historical drama. Concerns about the moral complexities inherent in deportation were not yet on my mental radar screen.

There was, I realized, also the prospect of family secrets spilling out from their long-sequestered spots. But these thoughts were not uppermost in my mind. All that mattered to me as I pondered joining forces with OSI was that I do whatever my generation could do to bear witness to history, to create an indelible record of atrocity and collaboration, and to exact justice.

Paula Gerson, born Peshka Szajt, and sisters in Zamość in 1924.

Chapter Two

Zamość: Poland's Urban Gem, My Ancestral Home

They lived in Zamość, a small town in southeast Poland, and they met at the Purim Ball on March 3, 1933—the four threes made the date easy to remember.

Peshka Szajt, my mother, at age 24 was a stylish five-foot-seven brunette who owned her own dressmaker studio, favored bold jackets and lace veils, and catered to the most affluent women in town. Mottel Gerzon, my father, was the same height as Peshka and three years older, with light blonde hair, wire-rimmed glasses, and a lean but muscular build. He managed his father's candy store as a self-taught bookkeeper; he was also a leader in Zionist and labor organizations.

Both Peshka and Mottel were educated, belonged to large families, and bore distinctive physical traits: Peshka had a space between her two front teeth, a chronic diastema, while Mottel was born with a "double thumb" on his left hand. Like all Jews in Zamość, (pronounced zah-MOsh), they came from religiously observant families, speaking Yiddish exclusively at home. Their parents demanded it. Whenever someone spoke Polish in Peshka's house, her father, who went to *shul* every night after work, yelled, "Polish is on the street! In the home I want Yiddish!" He became even angrier when someone spoke Polish on Shabbat.

Over the years, Peshka had seen Mottel walking on the streets and in the park, but the two had never spoken, not until 3/3/33. Peshka went to the Purim Ball with one of her sisters, and the sister introduced the two. The attraction was immediate. At night's end, Mottel asked Peshka, "Who would you like to take you home?"

Peshka said, "You." And they were gone.

They actually lived on the same street near the town center.

They both lived with their families and didn't have telephones, so either Peshka or Mottel just showed up at the other's apartment. The courtship progressed, the months passed, and then the years, but Mottel would not propose. One of his three older sisters had not yet married, and, according to Jewish custom, had Mottel married before her, he would put that sister to shame.

Peshka waited four years. Then she issued an ultimatum. This apparently coincided with Mottel's sister finding a match of her own. Mottel was free to marry with everyone's blessing, and on August 14, 1937, the couple exchanged vows in the apartment of Peshka's parents. She had made herself a white summer dress, with a small flower and a white hat. There was no rabbi and no elaborate ceremony. They signed a *ketuba*, or a marriage contract, sang and danced, and ate a nice meal prepared by neighbors.

Peshka and Mottel were devoted to each other and their families but also to Zamość, which at the time had about 28,000 residents, 12,000 of whom were Jews, who lived primarily in the center of the city. But this was no drab *shtetl* occupied by peasants with pushcarts on the rolling hills of central Europe. It was a visionary gem, founded in the 16th century by a Polish nobleman, Zamoyski, who had been educated in Italy and wanted to bring humanist values to his homeland. Zamość was located on a trade route that connected Western and Northern Europe to the Black Sea, and it became a commercial center as well as a cultural and academic hub.

The town was designed by Italian architect Bernardo Morando, in accordance to the Renaissance principles of the "Ideal City." That meant a checkerboard street layout, sophisticated town planning, and the construction of the Great Market Square surrounded by arcaded houses with vibrant facades and highlighted by the Town Hall, whose spires hovered majestically above, each topped with a lantern. The strategic location of Zamość, in the crosshair of empires, made it vulnerable to attacks. Its massive brick fortress, however, built at the turn of 16th century and surrounding the city, resisted half a dozen sieges, until advances in warfare made the fortress obsolete. But the town's protective tunnels, which included fireplaces and a bread oven, offered sanctuary against raids well into the future.

The founders of Zamość, in the spirit of tolerance, invited settlers from other nationalities and non-Catholic denominations, including Jews, the first of whom arrived from Spain in 1588. They were granted equal rights, including the right to own houses, build a brick synagogue, construct a *mikveh*, the ritual bath, and to establish a cemetery. The number of Sephardic Jews diminished over time, and in the 17th century they were replaced by Ashkenazi Jews, who had fled anti-Jewish massacres in Ukraine. These residents were entrepreneurial, opening businesses in grain, timber, and cattle, while other Jews became locksmiths and carpenters as well as scholars and sages.

Over the centuries, however, Jewish life was repeatedly threatened by invasions, occupations, and crackdowns. Under Russian rule in the 1830s, the Jews of Zamość were prohibited from entering the town center and were threatened with expulsion. They faced even greater oppression following the Russian revolution in 1905, with some Jews arrested or deported to Siberia. At the beginning of the First World War, when the Russian army recaptured Zamość after being briefly occupied by the Austro-Hungarian army, the Russians accused the Jews of collaboration and executed 11 of them. Poland re-emerged as an independent country in 1918, after which Polish Jews had to face abuses only from their own government.

Through it all, the Jewish community in Zamość survived and even flourished. My father called it "the jewel in the crown of Polish Jewry," the birthplace of several of his own heroes: Rosa Luxemburg, the Marxist anti-war revolutionary who was murdered in 1919 in Berlin for her political beliefs; and I.L. Peretz, one of the great writers of Yiddish literature, after whom Zamość named a public library.

Mottel's love for Yiddish and Hebrew poetry began early in life, at school, where he loved the rhythmic tones of the liturgy and where the alphabetically ordered psalms and prayers so captivated him that he would often write to special friends beginning the first sentences with the *aleph bet* and running through the alphabet through the rest of the letter. To him, poetry was a triumph of form over matter, a balance to the world of bookkeeping that occupied his daytime work.

Zamość had one *shul*, built in a mixture of Renaissance and Baroque styles. The *shul* adhered to the strict orthodoxy of men and women praying in separate rooms. Jewish political parties, associations, and newspapers thrived, along with schools. Jews had their own social service organizations that helped those who were ill or without food, clothing, or medicine, a business organization that offered loans without interest, and a spa outside of town offering their own retreat.

Before the Second World War, Jews controlled nearly 80 percent of the local trade in Zamość, according to the Holocaust Research Project. The men worked mostly as merchants or in the trades, as carpenters, tailors, shoemakers, locksmiths, butchers, and storekeepers. The women were seamstresses, as all shirts, pants, jackets, dresses, hats, and accessories were custom-made. It was not a rich community, but the men walked proudly in their double-breasted suits while the women showcased their fashionable jackets, white gloves, polka dot kerchiefs, and fedoras, tilted jauntily to the side.

Life in Zamość was still tenuous, with primitive medical care and public health. Peshka's parents had lost their first two children as infants, so they gave their third child, a boy, the middle name *Chaim*, or life, as if that name would spare him the fate as his siblings. Chaim did enjoy a healthy childhood.

As a young girl, Peshka was captivated not only by fashion, but also by style and design. Her favorite holiday was *Pesach*, in part because she loved the decorative dishes. She also marveled at the Great Market Square, not only for its colorful frontages and bas-relief figures, but for its role as a commercial and social center. She knew where her professional future lay. Jobs were scarce in Zamość, and women had few opportunities. By the time Peshka was a teenager, she was a good seamstress and worked for a dressmaker, but she wanted more.

When she was 19, Peshka told her parents that she wanted to attend the eminent Warsaw Design School to learn skills that no one taught in Zamość. Her parents objected. Very few women received an advanced degree, and fewer still traveled so far on their own. Warsaw was 160 miles away.

Her father asked, "Who lets his child go to another world?"

But Peshka was determined. "If I have to continue this trade," she said, "I want to be the best."

Her mother was more supportive. She had been orphaned as a young girl, never went to school, and never learned to read or write. "I am blind," she would say, "but I will do my best to make sure my children aren't blind."

Peshka's parents consented to her going, and she moved to Warsaw and lived with relatives, attending classes in the evening and working for a dressmaker during the day. After a year, she returned to Zamość, bought a table, a mirror, and a closet, and opened her own atelier in the bedroom of her parents' apartment. She soon hired several assistants as well. Her dresses, hats, and coats were more expensive than those of her peers—she said those were the prices in Warsaw—and her customers had to climb two flights of steps to reach her studio. But those clients, most of whom were non-Jewish—the wives of doctors, lawyers, and government officials—made the effort for access to the finest European fashions.

Mottel had also traveled beyond Zamość, but for very different reasons. He left town as a boy in 1914 with his parents and three sisters when the Eastern front of the war was closing in. They moved to Ukraine and then to Kiev, but they could hardly insulate themselves. Not only did they witness fighting between the Ukrainians and the Bolsheviks, but they also saw attacks against Jews, which intensified after the Russian revolution in 1917. In one particularly vicious assault, the Cossacks dragged a man with a beard through the streets of Kiev. Mottel learned early how easily the Jews were scapegoated for the troubles of the world.

His family returned to Zamość in 1919, and Mottel taught himself bookkeeping skills so he could work in and ultimately manage his father's candy store. His organizational abilities also put him in leadership roles with Zionist and labor groups that, by the 1930s, were increasingly motivated by threats from Germany, tumult in the Soviet Union, and hardships from a global Depression.

As children and young adults, both Peshka and Mottel knew of anti-Semitism in Zamość, but it was rarely dangerous. Peshka had gentile friends at her public school, which was almost entirely gentile. Mottel rarely encountered gentiles, as he attended Jewish schools and managed a store that served mostly Jewish patrons. The couple, who moved into their own apartment after they married, read the Polish as well as Yiddish newspapers, and like most of the Jews in Zamość, were keenly aware of Hitler's ascendance and the growing persecution against German Jews, including the horrors of *Kristallnacht* in 1938.

That year brought the menace of Nazism home for Polish Jews: In 1938, Hitler deported German Jews of Polish descent, including families that had been there for several generations. The Polish government initially refused to accept the deportees, though it ultimately relented. The influx resulted in Jewish refugee camps across the country. The Jews in Zamość formed teams to send food, clothes, and supplies to the newcomers.

The atmosphere was darkening in Zamość as well. Jews were more frequently harassed or bullied on the streets, and the police ignored their complaints. Arbitrary taxes were imposed on Jewish goods, and signs were posted not to buy anything from Jews. Peshka was operating her dressmaking store from her apartment. One Sunday morning, while she was working, a policeman knocked and gave her a citation for breaking a new law that prohibited any business from being open on a Sunday. Jewish businesses were closed on Shabbat, or Friday evening to Saturday evening, and many of those businesses, including Peshka's, reopened on Sunday. Peshka went to court, where a judge told her that she could either pay the fine (the equivalent of two dresses) or stand trial. "You better pay the fine," he said, "because if you go to trial, who are they going to listen to? You, a Jewish girl, or a gentile policeman?"

Peshka paid the fine, but the harassment didn't end. She had long employed three or four seamstresses, but in 1939 she was told that a new law required that she have one gentile employee for every two Jewish employees. She held off complying, but events soon made the injunction, as well as all other laws and regulations, irrelevant.

Allan Gerson with his mentor from Yale Law School, Eugene Rostow, in 1981.

Chapter Three

Rockler, Rostow, Talleyrand and "Zeal"

Walter Rockler, the new director of the Office of Special Investigations, gave me a week—until Wednesday, May 23, 1979—to decide whether to accept his offer to join the unit as its first trial attorney. I realized it would be a leap in the dark, yet another professional incarnation. Joan had misgivings, but I knew that in the end she would support whatever path I took. Still, I needed help to make sure that it wasn't a flight of fancy, that the road would not culminate in a dead end.

I decided to ask some friends and acquaintances whose opinions I valued highly, and first on my list was Benjamin Ferencz, a former Nuremberg prosecutor who had tried 24 leaders of *Einsatzgruppen*, the paramilitary death squads. Fourteen were sentenced to death by hanging and two were given life sentences. Ferencz became a respected lawyer in New York, his main ambition to establish reparations and rehabilitation programs for Holocaust survivors and to advance the rule of law. It was in his latter pursuit that we met frequently at American Society of International Law functions and established a warm friendship.

When I asked Ferencz for his views on my joining OSI, he said: "I recommend you for the job, but not the job itself." I understood what he meant. At Nuremberg, he prosecuted Nazis who had overseen such operations as the massacre at Babi Yar, in which 33,771 Jews were killed in two days.

Now I'd be prosecuting the lowest rung of those who had facilitated the Final Solution. Was that, Ben seemed to imply, the best use of American financial and moral capital? And was it worthy of my time? If Benjamin Ferencz's half-endorsement was intended as a warning bell, I managed not to hear it.

I next took a train to New Haven, Connecticut, to meet with my former thesis adviser at Yale, Gene Rostow; his own background seemed perfectly suited to assess the merits of OSI's planned denaturalizations and deportations of Nazi collaborators living in America.

Rostow, named for Eugene V. Debs, the American Socialist, with whom he shared Debs' zeal if not his politics (entirely), had been an early and harsh critic of the incarceration of Japanese Americans during the Second World War. In 1945, as a newly tenured Yale professor, Rostow published a brilliant and courageous article in the *Yale Law Journal* in which he cast as 'racist' the US Supreme Court's decision validating President Franklin D. Roosevelt's order to incarcerate Japanese Americans on the West Coast. Rostow, known for his courtly ways, didn't mince words in castigating Roosevelt's order as one that "violates every democratic social value."

A self-described "New England Puritan Jew," he was dean of Yale Law School from 1955 to 1965 and was widely admired for propelling it to international renown. When his older brother, Walt (named after Walt Whitman), became national security adviser to President Lyndon B. Johnson, he lured Gene to join the administration as undersecretary for political affairs. Walt was one of the architects of the Vietnam War, and Gene's ardent support of the war would make him a magnet for critics.

When Rostow returned to his beloved Yale in 1969, students booed him in the halls. Although his office was adjacent to the Sterling Law Library, he no longer ventured in for fear of creating a disturbance. Instead, he asked the library staff to cart back and forth the manifold number of books he was consuming as he began writing on his last great topic: the problems of bringing law to bear on an uncivilized world.

My first communication with Rostow was in 1971. At the time I was a graduate student at the Hebrew University of Jerusalem, where I had been asked if I would write a review of an intriguing new book. Its author was Michael V. Reisman, a young professor of international law who had worked closely at Yale with one of the giants in the field, Professor Myres S. McDougal. The book, *The Art of the Possible*, made proposals—some of them retreads of older attempts, and some stunningly new—for resolving the Arab-Israeli conflict. I gave it a complimentary but less-than-gushing review (it was my first published scholarly piece). Knowing of Gene Rostow's interest in the subject, I forwarded to him a copy of the review. I hadn't anticipated the response. Rostow sent a long, thoughtful handwritten note, complimenting me for the balanced way I had handled the review. I was taken by it, and in turn considered it a prompt to apply to Yale's doctoral (JSD) international law program.

I was accepted, and by the time I arrived at Yale in 1972, campus tensions had eased considerably (the draft would end the following year). Rostow had returned to teaching, offering a seminar on international law and the use of force. I was one of his students, and I also chose him as my thesis adviser on my project: Israel's military occupation of the West Bank.

What followed were many unforgettable sessions with Rostow. He was always well turned out, sartorially resplendent in bespoke English three-piece suits. His warm, intelligent, large brown eyes would bear down on me as I explained whatever it was that I was trying to accomplish. Somehow, he seemed to have all the time in the world for me.

Eugene Rostow, more than anyone I had ever met, believed that if America was true to its mission of a world order based on the rule of law, like America's conduct of domestic policy but based on the principles imbedded in the UN Charter, achievement of world peace was indeed within our grasp. In this sense, one might say he differed little from Woodrow Wilson and his *14 Points* for a post-Word War I world, or from Franklin Roosevelt and Harry Truman. Each had been devoted to creating a universally accepted UN Charter, and each had been convinced it was the indispensable guide to charting a way out of the cycle of wars plaguing the planet, each more devastating than the last. But Rostow took it a step further, and was more zealous in his application: there had to be a price to be paid by aggressors, large and small, if deterrence was our guiding principle. This was the lodestar of his convictions under its command. That is why he saw America as justifiably, and proudly, in Vietnam. Lines *had to be drawn,* he would insist, and a marker laid down to North Vietnam for its support of the paramilitary forces infiltrating its neighbor, South Vietnam.

The tragedy, as I increasingly came to view it, was that once Rostow saw high principles violated—principally, the commitment to non-use of force except in self-defense—he accorded little room for balancing the costs and benefits of resort to arms. Little wonder that he detested the *realpolitik* of Henry Kissinger, who viewed statecraft as infinitely flexible, subject to the exigencies (and opportunities) of the moment, and not bound by overriding principles. Therefore, while Kissinger gained accolades for negotiating the Paris Peace Accords that allowed our exit from Vietnam, Rostow seethed that it was a betrayal of our commitment to the rule of law and was bound to foreshadow negative consequences for America.

Thus Rostow became a tragic figure, booed in the halls of Yale, including catcalls as a war criminal, on his return from government service. This did not diminish my admiration for the man, but only heightened my awareness of the pitfalls of zeal even in the most virtuous of endeavors. This was doubly ironic, as Rostow had a tendency to cite, and ignore, the immortal quote of the renowned 18th century French statesman and diplomat, Charles Maurice de Talleyrand: "Above all, not too much zeal."

But it wasn't Rostow's abiding belief in the rule of law in the conduct of foreign relations that was of interest to me now. It was his insight into the human rights dimensions of the detention and trial of suspected collaborators with our country's enemies. I wanted it all distilled for purposes of deciding to take on the new job at OSI.

That was why, for my train ride up to New Haven, I had packed Rostow's famous article, "The Japanese American Cases—A Disaster" in the 1945 *Yale Law Journal*, in which he had castigated the decision to intern Japanese Americans in detention camps. Reading it, I was bowled over by the sheer power and elegance of his argument.

I underlined the key provisions as I read:

> The course of action which we undertook was in no way required or justified by the circumstance of the war. It was calculated to produce both individual injustice and deep-seated social maladjustments of a cumulative and sinister kind.
>
> Perhaps 70,000 persons are still in camps, "loyal" and "disloyal" citizens and aliens alike, more than three years after the program was instituted.
>
> The dominant factor in the development of this policy was not a military estimate of a military problem, but familiar West Coast attitudes of race prejudice.

That the Supreme Court has upheld imprisonment on such a basis…ignores the rights of citizenship, and the safeguards of trial practice which have been the historical safeguards of liberty.

I put down the piece. It was a stirring indictment of the actions of the most popular institutions in America—the US Supreme Court, and the presidency. The facts as he had coolly assembled them were unassailable. By this decision, America was ushering in two forms of citizenship, making the rights of Japanese Americans inferior to those of other American citizens.

I arrived at his home from Yale Station just in time to join him for his sherry hour at 4 p.m.

"Allan, it was good of you to come and see me," he said with a smile as he lit up a Pall Mall cigarette in the living room of his spacious home.

"Quite the other way around Professor Rostow, if I may say so. It was good of you to see *me*."

I had already explained on the phone that I was thinking of joining OSI as its first trial lawyer, and now I reminded him that our goal would be to strip naturalized Americans of their citizenship if they collaborated with the Nazis and lied about it on entering the country.

"Noble enterprise," Rostow said, "but fraught with danger. US citizenship is a precious commodity. Doesn't matter how it was acquired; they are all equal before the law. You know the Emma Goldman case, don't you?"

"Can't say I do, Sir," I said, feeling as if a law student, caught unprepared, in one of his classes.

"Well, *you should*. After World War I, the US government was using immigration law to deport *undesirables* – people they didn't like. A nasty business."

"I'll look it up right away."

Rostow told me to remember Talleyrand: "*Above all, no zeal*. Retribution is one thing, but they're now American citizens. You can never forget that."

"Yes, sir, I am aware of that." I was also mindful of the irony in the wake of our collective and individual Vietnam experience.

Rostow continued. "As you've already learned, transitioning

from academic life to government work is hard, hard precisely because you're giving up so much freedom. And if you're not on top making government policy, you face becoming a cog in a big machine. Don't think that's your style."

"It's generous of you to say that."

Rostow referenced an article I had recently published in the *Harvard International Law Journal*—"Trustee-Occupant: The Legal Status of Israel's Presence in the West Bank."

"Very innovative," he said.

"Thank you."

"But innovation has its drawbacks. It's not rewarded in the ranks. Maybe you'll have a chance to shape things in this new job, to teach them about the rule of law."

Rostow asked me about Walter Rockler and what I knew of him.

I told him I didn't know much, except that he had done the Bankers case at Nuremberg and that he was now a successful tax lawyer. "He seems sincere enough," I said, "in wanting to use the law to establish a record of what these collaborators did and then deporting them."

Rostow reiterated that furthering respect for the rule of law would have to be an essential component of the job. "It's our only hope for civilization," he said. "Freud had it right in *Civilization and its Discontents*: we are not born angels. It will be your job to get that across."

I told Rostow that I had just re-read his 1945 article criticizing the Japanese American internment camps. "Brilliant," I said, "and so courageous at the time."

He thanked me and noted that Japanese Americans were then the least popular group in the country. "Took a long while for the Supreme Court to realize the error of its ways," he said, "but the damage was done. Holmes was right: 'The law grinds infinitely slow but infinitely fine.' Sometimes."

We had finished our sherry, and he smiled and patted me on the back.

Come Wednesday morning, a dutiful secretary ushered me into Rockler's office, where he was sitting hunched behind his desk, presiding over scattered papers, a large crystal ashtray to his right already half-filled with ground-out cigarette butts.

Catching sight of me, he put aside his large eyeglasses and, pulling up his lumbering frame, unaccountably larger than it had seemed the week before, he rose to greet me, his handshake again honing in on the fleshy ridge between my thumb and forefinger, grasping me as if a comrade-in-arms. He pointed me to one of the two comfortable armchairs near the corner next to the window. Now the setting was more intimate than before. Situated between our two facing chairs was a small glass cocktail table, another ashtray to the side, and in the center of the table, as if on display, was an old bound brief with a fading red cover inscribed: *"US Prosecution Brief: The Bankers Case, Nuremberg War Crimes Trials Commission."*

I knew the case even though it was not common knowledge, even among the international law cognoscenti; it had been a sort of afterthought at Nuremberg, following the completion of the regular trials of major Nazi war criminals. Unknown to Rockler, I had much more than a passing interest in Nuremberg.

When I was studying at Yale, I spent my days entombed in a tiny carrel in its subterranean international law library. The claustrophobic environment was made all the worse because in my prior space, at the Hebrew University, my small desk and cubicle had faced the whole vista of New Jerusalem, Old Jerusalem, and the Dead Sea beyond. At Yale, I was literally underground in tight, windowless quarters. These conditions were redeemed, though, with a cache of documents by my carrel from the Nuremberg trials: the judgments, along with some briefs and introductions. The trials themselves, from November 20, 1945, to October 1, 1946, had accused 22 Nazis of war crimes, and the proceedings resulted in the convictions of 12 defendants who were sentenced to die by hanging and seven defendants who were sentenced to prison. Three were acquitted. I studied the documents, bound in light blue, with awe and fascination, particularly the opening poetic and visionary statement of US Supreme Court Justice Robert Jackson, the original chief US prosecutor:

> The wrongs which we seek to condemn and punish have been so calculated, so malignant, and so devastating, that civilization cannot tolerate their being ignored, because it cannot survive their being repeated. That four great nations, flushed with victory and stung with injury, stay the hand of

vengeance and voluntarily submit their captive enemies to the judgment of the law is one of the most significant tributes that power has ever paid to reason.

Nuremberg represented the apotheosis of bringing the rule of law to bear on international affairs and gave meaning to my study of international law: It wasn't an abstraction; it was real, it established precedent. If it in fact deterred similar behavior, it could make the difference between war and peace; with those bound copies in my little Yale dungeon, I reveled in the tactile proof of Nuremberg's greatness.

The so-called Bankers Case, which Rockler prosecuted, wasn't technically part of Nuremberg. It took place a year later, in 1947, its goal to prosecute the financiers of the Third Reich. Dresdner Bank in particular was implicated for underwriting the SS, bankrolling the arms sector, and seizing Jewish property. Dresdner officials were found guilty, but their sentences were commuted.

Rockler reached for a Camel out of his soft pack, tapped it two or three times in his palm, and offered me one. I declined. He lit it, inhaled deeply, and exhaled slowly.

"So, what have you decided?"

"To take the job," I said, "but there are things that I would like to go over first, if I may."

"Shoot."

"You said, last time, that I don't exactly fit the profile of what you are looking for. I have no real criminal experience. So…"

He cut me short: "That's okay. Like I said, this isn't going to be Nuremberg. We'll be using US immigration law to get them. So it will be a hell of a lot easier than learning how to handle a criminal trial. Heymann must have told you that."

"Yes, sir. I understand that."

"We just have to demonstrate," Rockler continued, that "it was more likely than not" that the Nazi collaborators did what they are accused of, lying on their visa applications about having "assisted" in persecution.

"That's the language of the statute," he said. "If you *'assisted,'* you're not eligible for entry into America. Period. End of story. Not like Nuremberg at all."

"I understand you were there, for the last trial. The Bankers Case."

"Heymann tell you that?"

"Yes, he did, and I did a little research of my own, Sir."

"Hey, this isn't the Army. No need for the '*Sirs.*'"

"*Yes, Sir.* I mean, Yes, Mr. Rockler."

Rockler interrupted me, as if putting two and two together. "We got the bankers then, and I want to get these scum now. Don't get me wrong. My wife is German, met her right after the war. Now I want to get those like the banker bastards who never had to pull a trigger but enabled countless others to do it."

"What was it like in Germany, at Nuremberg, so soon after the war? If I may ask."

"The Germans we had to prosecute were about your age. Strapping fellows, blond-haired, blue-eyed guys like you," he said. "Your family must have had some Crusader blood mixed up in it. But I didn't answer your question, Allan. What was it like in Germany back then? Frankly, it's the way I like to remember it: *Rubble and smoldering ruins*. The Russians wanted to shoot the Nazis we captured. But Roosevelt wanted to teach the world about this rule of law thing, give them fair trials, and set down a record of everything the bastards did. Suppose he was right. History will be the judge."

I shifted uncomfortably, as his body language seemed to suggest that perhaps the Russians, and Churchill, were right: that the elaborate ritual of a war crimes tribunal on a grand scale had been misplaced.

"I know what you're thinking," he said. "Don't get me wrong. I'm not knocking Nuremberg. After all, I did the Bankers Case."

Peshka Gerzon holds her first-born son, Erik, in 1938. The baby died the next year of diphtheria as they fled the Nazis.

Chapter Four

Pawns in a Transcontinental Struggle

On August 23, 1939, Nazi Germany and the Soviet Union signed a nonaggression pact, which defined spheres of influence for the two powers, each controlling specific countries but splitting Poland in two. Without fear of Soviet resistance, Germany invaded Poland nine days later, on September 1, sending armored divisions across the border, launching bombing raids on cities and airfields, and deploying warships and U-boats against Poland's navy in the Baltic Sea. The attack itself came as little surprise, as Hitler had already annexed Czechoslovakia and had made his territorial ambitions clear. But the Polish army was quickly overwhelmed. Little wonder: it was sending cavalrymen on horses against German tanks, and so its troops were systematically captured or killed. Thousands of civilians died in air raids on Warsaw, and German forces reached the capital city in eight days.

The first bombs fell on Zamość on September 2, damaging a number of structures, but the residents found shelter in buildings and tunnels. Zamość had faced attacks for more than 300 years, and for all they knew, this was just one more. Still, Peshka and Mottel had more reason than most to be worried: their firstborn, Eric, was six weeks old. He had been delivered in their apartment with the assistance of a midwife. For Eric's *bris*, the ritual circumcision, they struggled finding enough men for a *minyan* to do the blessings, the requisite 10, because so many were registering for the army.

The German bombing of Zamość lasted only one day, and once England and France entered the war on September 3, most in town believed that the war would not last long—a few weeks, maybe a month or two. The German troops arrived in Zamość in the second week of September, and their occupation began. Stores were shut down. Soldiers manned the streets. Martial law was imposed.

Then the world tilted again.

On September 17, the Soviet Union invaded Poland from the east, another battering ram to a wounded body. The Red Army faced little resistance, and the Polish government fled south, evacuating to Romania one day after the invasion. Poland was split asunder by two hostile powers, with Zamość tucked just inside German territory.

The Nazis had been in Zamość for less than two weeks when Peshka, walking down a street, said something in German to a soldier. "Don't talk German now," he said. "You better learn Russian, because the Russians are coming."

According to the non-aggression pact that Germany and the Soviet Union had signed, Zamość was part of the Soviet sphere, which was why the Germans rolled out of town and were promptly replaced by the Red Army. For the Jews of Zamość, this was seen as a gift from heaven. Unlike the well-equipped Germans, the Russian soldiers were a rag-tag group, with frayed and mismatched uniforms. Furthermore, many of the Jews in Zamość were either Communists or belonged to workers' unions. In the Russians they saw possible allies, not occupants, and the soldiers obliged by re-opening the stores and inching the town back to normalcy.

Then came the announcement, from the fan-like steps of Town Hall, that the German-Soviet border in Poland had been changed yet again. Incredibly, Zamość would be returning to the Nazis. It was as if this one little town in Poland was part of some geopolitical tug of war. The new boundary was the Bug River (pronounced Boog), less than 25 miles to the east, shallow enough to wade across in some places, but with swirling whitewater rapids in others. The Russians would soon be leaving.

If the Jews were naïve about the Soviets, they had no illusions about the Germans. Panic swept through the community, driven by rumors that the Nazis would deport the young men to labor camps and, without adequate food, starve them. Mottel decided to flee, and he would become part of an exodus of Jews to leave Zamość, about 5,000 in all, mostly young, male, and politically active (and including one of Mottel's brothers-in-law). Mottel was certain that his absence would be brief because the war would be over soon. He took one knapsack, and when Peshka gave him three shirts, he objected.

"Why do I need more than one shirt?" he asked. "When I get on the other side, I'll get a job and buy some more shirts." He assured her that nothing would happen to the women or the children of Zamość.

The Russians were still in Zamość when Mottel fled, crossing the Bug River and stopping at a town called Vlodzimersh. There, he soon found shelter in churches, synagogues, and schools, but Peshka was instantly heartsick. She could not imagine being separated from Mottel under any circumstance, but particularly now, with a newborn. Shortly after he had left, she was standing in the town square, and Russian trucks suddenly roared by, with soldiers scurrying about. They were leaving, but they had one more announcement.

"Anyone who wants to come with us can do so, but you can't take any belongings."

Peshka raced to her parents' apartment, where she and her baby were now staying. She told them that the Russians would take any travelers, and she was going to leave with her son to be with Mottel.

Her father was livid. Two of his sons had already moved to Argentina, where job prospects were better, and had never returned, and he feared the same would happen with Peshka. Word had already arrived in Zamość that this first town on the other side of the Bug River had people living on the streets. It lacked food, water, and was suffering outbreaks of disease, including dysentery. If Peshka's going to Warsaw for design school was unacceptable, this was truly unthinkable.

"Where are you going with the baby?" he demanded.

"To be with his father," Peshka said.

"*You will lose the baby!*" he shouted through his tears.

But Peshka insisted that she would only be gone for a few months. She packed a bag and two diapers and, carrying her baby, headed for an open army truck. She had two sisters, and one of them raced after her, begging to join her. Peshka told her no. She needed to stay with their parents.

It was October 5, a warm evening. Peshka had already stocked her apartment for the winter with wood, coal, and potatoes, and her mother assured her that she would look after things until she returned.

On October 7, the Germans barreled back into Zamość, and the Jews immediately had their property looted and their movement restricted. They couldn't use their cars or leave town. They were also ordered to wear a white armband with a yellow Star of David. The Germans formed a *Judenrat*, a council of Jewish elders, who helped them administer the ghetto.

Peshka and Eric somehow managed to unite with Mottel in Vlodzimersh, and they lived in a church, sharing a room with one of Mottel's sisters and brother-in-law, who had also fled with the Russians. Information was scarce, but they soon realized that, even with the entrance of England and France, the war would not be ending quickly. Winter arrived, and in December the Russians announced that the refugees were too close to the German border and would have to move farther east. Border towns are strategic positions, and Mottel assumed they had to vacate to make room for more Russian soldiers. The move would take them farther from Zamość, but they were given no choice.

They boarded a train and traveled to Lviv, a much larger city in western Ukraine, known for its industry, science, and culture, but now occupied by the Russian army. Still other members of Mottel's family who had left Zamość, including his two sisters, their husbands, and his cousins, joined Peshka and Mottel there. While Lviv was a relatively advanced city and already had a significant Jewish population, conditions proved to be worse. Their apartment was small and often not heated, and the weather was bitter cold, the coldest that Peshka had ever experienced. She prayed that if she could live until May, she could take her son outside again, and they would be saved.

The city was in tumult. Since the start of the war, Lviv had attracted thousands of Jewish Polish refugees who were escaping the Germans, but that imposed food and housing shortages and created other strains. One time, Mottel arrived at a supermarket at 4 a.m. and stood in line until 8 a.m., at which point the manager announced the store was out of meat and bread. Mottel had to find provisions on the black market, and it was there that he found a sewing machine for Peshka, which allowed her to make additional clothes for the family while selling other items on the black market.

In these conditions, perhaps it was inevitable that Eric developed a cough, and perhaps it was inevitable that he couldn't shake it. A doctor from Zamość, now a refugee, was summoned, and the baby was taken to a hospital with Peshka. Eric had developed diphtheria, a bacterial infection. A vaccine had been developed and by 1940 was widely used, but it was not available in the man-swarm of Lviv. May arrived, and just as Peshka had hoped, the days lengthened and the weather warmed. But that wasn't enough. Eric died before he saw his first birthday, in the hospital. Peshka went into a rage and had to be escorted out the doors, leaving the body behind. There was never a funeral. When Peshka returned home, Mottel said her hair had gone directly from graying to white, and for the rest of her life, Peshka would remember her father's warning that "you will lose the baby."

The weeks that followed Eric's death marked another turning point for all Polish refugees, a large percentage of whom were in Lviv.

Since Germany's invasion of Poland, hundreds of thousands of Polish citizens had fled east and lived under Soviet occupation, including tens of thousands of Jews. By June 1940, Soviet rule had become increasingly oppressive, yet the Germans were entrenched in Poland. Rare in history has a single group of people, particularly the Jews, been faced with such a barbarous choice—life (or death) under Stalin, or under Hitler. Most of the refugees, Jews and non-Jews, thought that Stalin would outlast Hitler and therefore was the worse choice. They also wanted to return home, to German-occupied Poland, and the Russians took advantage of their eagerness.

In early 1940, claiming they wanted information on who wanted to return to Poland, the Russians distributed registries to the Poles in Lviv, and they promised to make possible their return. Ninety-five percent of the Poles signed up, including 80 percent of the Jews. The first departures occurred in June, with alarms sounding at night, trucks rolling down the streets, and trains at the ready. In fact, the Poles had no choice but to go, but the Russians announced that the refugees would be returning home, diminishing the odds of any resistance. The men were the first to leave, with soldiers going door to door to bring them to the station.

But Mottel had heard about the worsening conditions in Zamość under the Nazis, and he did not want to return. He figured he could stay clear of the Russians by hiding in a factory.

The Russians next began sending entire families, and on June 10, soldiers arrived at Peshka's apartment. Still traumatized from the recent death of her son, she was not about to be separated from Mottel. "My husband's not here," she said. "You can bring him, but alone I'm not going."

Also in the apartment was Mottel's brother-in-law, Shimon, who took the soldiers to Mottel and brought him home. The couple was united and joined by six members of Mottel's family: two sisters (Ruchsa and Chuma) and their husbands, including Shimon; and one brother (Moishe) and his wife (Rushka). They headed for the train, but after they reached the street, Peshka asked the soldier if she could retrieve an item: her sewing machine. The soldier agreed. Peshka knew that if she had her sewing machine, she wouldn't starve.

They spent the whole day at the station, until the train rumbled in and the doors opened. Night fell, and the men, women, and children, Jews and non-Jews, secular and religious, were pressed into cars that were otherwise occupied by cattle. The doors were shut and locked, the whistle sounded. The passengers were crammed together, about 100 per car, with no place to sit, sealed in darkness. Some screamed. Others held tight. The cab lurched, and the wheels began to churn. Then fear was followed by panic. The train was not heading west and was not returning to Poland. It was chugging north, heading deeper into Soviet territory.

There was no place to sleep or even sit, except the floor. The train stopped in the morning, at another station, and the passengers were given some bread and soup, consisting of dried tomato peels and water. And they were off again. Window slats allowed for some fresh air and sunlight, but the second day brought an even greater menace—lice, which had been attached comfortably to the cattle but now clutched the humans. The cars had a hole in the floor for a toilet. Otherwise, the passengers waited for stops in the countryside. There was no effort to flee because there was no place to escape. In one instance, a boy drifted off, and the train pulled away before he could jump back on. His mother later wrote letters to Stalin.

The refugees had a new status—they were now the deported, and they had become pawns in a transcontinental struggle between two powers. They still didn't know where they were going, not on this train or any of the other trains that had left occupied territories. But they were fanning out, deeper into the Soviet Union, passing Kiev and Minsk and Moscow, and farther still. The more miles they traveled, the fewer restrictions they faced. At some stations the passengers brought back pots of hot water or even visited a market and traded their watches or other items. While the train was in motion, some doors were left open, and the kids sat with their legs out and sang to kill time. Days passed, the green countryside rolled by, but the mood remained bleak. It appeared to Peshka that the non-Jewish men were educated professionals, perhaps deemed a greater threat to the Russians. When one such man, an engineer, began reading a book to his young boy, his wife snapped, "Why are you teaching him to read now? Why don't you teach him to become a shepherd?"

Meanwhile, as the train entered more remote areas, Mottel saw some of the gulags, or forced labor camps, and he thought that the Soviet Union would someday implode from within: No country could do this to its own people and survive, he told me often as I was growing up. Other than my father, no one seemed to be advancing the idea that one day the Soviet Union would implode from within, and I can't say I took it seriously back then.

Eventually, the Russians used train stops to unlatch cars, leaving them and their passengers behind, and then moving on. Those still traveling didn't realize that their train had gotten shorter until the next stop. Where any one person dropped off, in whatever district, subdivision, or town, in Kotlas or Samara, Chelyabinsk or Omsk, was randomly determined: your train, your car, was your destiny.

Regardless, they were all taken to labor camps, somewhere in the harsh, sprawling land mass of Siberia.

Fyodor Fedorenko lied about his Nazi past to enter the United States. Following a Supreme Court verdict he was deported to the Soviet Union where he was executed.

Chapter Five

Rockler's Mind: Mired in the Past

My first day at OSI, on April 24, 1979, I met Walter Rockler at its new quarters: a rented second-floor suite in an imposing prewar building in downtown Washington. The offices were directly above a Kentucky Fried Chicken outlet, and perhaps because the ductwork was not fully sealed, the smell of rancid fried oil wafted up to the second floor. It didn't help that we had to keep the windows locked in deference to Department of Justice security concerns. It was as if we had to keep the outside world from distracting us so that we might fully focus on the atrocities of another generation. That put us in a time warp. Outside in the early morning light, Fourteenth and K Streets were littered with the detritus of the night before: condoms, discarded needles, and small empty packets that formed the drug and prostitution trade. Inside, it was the 1940s, dossiers on death camps neatly placed on our desks for review and recommendations.

Rockler introduced me to Martin Mendelsohn, the head of the INS unit that had been looking into charges of Nazi collaborators in America. A close ally of Congresswoman Holtzman, Mendelsohn would be Rockler's deputy, and he was there to inspect the new offices. Though located just a short distance from Pennsylvania Avenue, where the massive Justice Department building was located, the separate location of OSI hinted that the Criminal Division preferred to keep the unit at a distance. Mendelsohn, a political operative, having worked on Capitol Hill for many years, surely knew this.

With Rockler at his side, he came to my desk with a stack of case files. "Here, Allan," he said. "Mr. Rockler said that you might want to get acquainted with this."

He handed me a thick binder marked "Fedor Fedorenko." He was a former Nazi death camp guard at Treblinka, now 72 years old and retired in Miami Beach, and DOJ was trying to strip him of his citizenship and deport him. A district court had blocked that effort, but the Third Circuit Court of Appeals reversed that ruling, which would pave the way for his deportation. But according to Mendelsohn, the US Supreme Court had just decided to grant *certiorari* and review the decision. "OSI's success may hinge on what they decide to do with this," Mendelsohn said.

Rockler nodded his head, but his body language suggested that he didn't take well to Mendelsohn, who was a glad-hander. Rockler didn't glad-hand. It appeared to me that Rockler brought him on as deputy as the political price he was paying for Rep. Holtzman's support.

Rockler also gave me the file to Wolodymir Osidach, who was now a 75-year-old retired slaughterhouse worker in Philadelphia.

"This is a good case to get started on," Rockler said. "I'll soon be hiring other attorneys, about 10, so you certainly won't be the only one doing this case. It's too important. It's OSI's first, besides Fedorenko, but that may be handled by Main Justice. They already got involved in it in the courts below."

Rockler said he also had material on one of Osidach's sidekicks, named Sarowycz (not his real name). "From what I have read of the file," he said, "Osidach was the police chief, and Sarowycz was his go-between with the SS as they liquidated the Jews—about 18,000 of them—in a town called Rawa-Ruska in western Ukraine. Just across the border from Poland."

Rockler told me that I had already been provisionally cleared, at least to begin my work, so I needed to get up to speed on Fedorenko while also preparing the Osidach case. He said he might be sending me out in a week to 10 days to depose some potential witnesses.

"I really want us to get started soon," he said. "You read me?"

He seemed glad to be issuing directives again, and I was glad to be taking them from him.

"Yes, sir," I said. "I'll get on it right away."

My caseload at Civil Appellate had been cleared, as I had just completed my last appellate argument. So without any hesitation I turned to the materials on *Fedorenko*. I was hooked, in more ways than one.

Before the war, Feodor Fedorenko had been a truck driver in a provincial Ukrainian town. He was recruited in 1941 to be part of a Ukrainian unit of the Soviet Army, but that unit was quickly decimated, and its remnants interned at the large German POW camp at Chelm, Poland. There, half of the 80,000 POWs died of starvation in the winter of 1941-42. Fedorenko survived and was sent to a training camp in Poland, and from there became a guard at various concentration camps, including Treblinka, where 800,000 Jews were murdered.

After the war, Fedorenko had made his way into the US zone of occupation in Germany, and he applied for an entry visa to the United States, thought he did not mention his Nazi guard duties on his application. The visa was granted, and arriving penniless in 1949, he settled in Waterbury, Connecticut, where he worked as a furnace operator at the Scovill Metal Works until he retired in 1973. He married an American woman as well—he assumed his wife had died in the war—and became a naturalized citizen. But in the early 1970s, he learned that his wife and son were in fact alive and living in the Soviet Union. That in turn prompted his three trips there to visit them. He went for two weeks in 1973, for three weeks in 1974, and for 51 weeks in 1975 and 1976. The last trip brought him to the attention of Soviet authorities, who questioned him at length about his service at Treblinka. They let him go but then gave word to a pro-Soviet weekly run out of a Manhattan tenement that he had been a Nazi collaborator. The weekly published the information, which not surprisingly found its way to the Justice Department and the INS. The INS agents found him living in Miami's South Beach area, where its pre-war art-deco glory was a thing of the past (and the future) and, at that time, a rather unpleasant place, largely populated by poor Jewish pensioners living out their years in crumbling hotels.

The agents had a simple question: had he been a guard at Treblinka? But it wasn't a simple question. Fedorenko recognized that it was probably no coincidence that the INS visit came in 1977, shortly after his return from the Soviet Union, and he surmised that the Russians were out to get him. He told the INS agents that he wanted the advice of counsel, and they acceded to his request. He chose Brian Gildea of Waterbury, Connecticut, who told him not to be concerned, that he had a perfect defense: that he never "assisted" in persecution because the role of a concentration camp guard had been thrust upon him, that he had no choice, that it was all involuntary, as he would have died of starvation had he refused the Germans' "offer."

As Congress was now increasingly agitated about the rumors of Nazis in America, Fedorenko's case received significant attention. Instead of being buried in the recesses of INS, the agency transferred it to the Office of the US Attorney for the Southern District of Florida, which filed a denaturalization complaint against Fedorenko, and in 1978 the case went to trial in Fort Lauderdale. With heightened media attention, passions ran high: The Jewish Defense League ran newspaper ads offering chartered buses from Miami to Fort Lauderdale, and demonstrators outside the courtroom chanted: "Who do we want? Fedorenko! How do we want him? Dead!" Protestors inside the courtroom were arrested as well.

Of greater substance was the actual testimony: Six survivors of Treblinka testified that Fedorenko had beaten or shot Jewish prisoners at the camp. A government witness also testified that after the war, an armed guard who was seeking to immigrate to America would have been ineligible for admission, even if he had been coerced into serving as a guard—he would still have been assisting in the persecution of civilians. Another witness testified that Fedorenko could have tried to escape Treblinka, as other guards had done so. The government's position was straightforward: Fedorenko had assisted the enemy and lied about it to enter America, so he should be stripped of his citizenship.

Testifying on his own behalf, he said that as a POW he survived on grass and roots and that he would have died had he not agreed to his training as a guard. At Treblinka itself, he said he knew that Jews were being murdered but as a perimeter guard, he had nothing to do with those deaths, and while he once shot in the direction of escaping prisoners, he did not aim to kill. He said he lied on his visa papers to avoid repatriation to the Soviet Union.

Fedorenko's lawyer argued that the DP Act encompassed only *voluntary* assistance. Otherwise, the Jews who had survived concentration camps who also twisted their identities to come here would be at risk themselves of losing their US citizenship and facing deportation. The same thing was true, Fedorenko's lawyer contended, of the Jews who had served as *kapos*.

In response, the US Attorney said that the text of the law never restricted the word "assisted" to purely voluntary assistance. Even *involuntary* acts, or coerced acts under duress, could be construed as assisting the enemy. Nonetheless, the government had to acknowledge that some things are implicit in the law, like implicit warranties against manufacturers' defects, and US criminal law generally does not penalize individuals for involuntary acts.

That left the US Attorney with arguing that immigration law was in a class by itself and that aliens (which Fedorenko was when he submitted his visa application) should not be the ones to be arguing about fine distinctions between the *implicit* and *explicit* intent of the law. At the same time, the US Attorney assured the court (and hopefully the concerned Jewish community beyond) that Jewish Holocaust survivors, who as musicians or *kapos* might have "assisted" the Nazis, would never be subjected, *as a matter of prosecutorial discretion*, to denaturalization and deportation proceedings based on that fact.

The judge was not convinced and ruled in Fedorenko's favor, concurring with the defense that stripping Fedorenko of his US citizenship regardless of intent would have the perverse result of endangering the citizenship of all Jewish Holocaust victims. To read the Displaced Persons Act of 1948, he wrote, as encompassing "any assistance, whether voluntary or involuntary, in connection with camp treatment of civilian populations" would bar from entry "every Jewish prisoner who survived Treblinka because each assisted the SS in the operation of the camp. Each did so involuntarily and under the utmost distress. For example, working prisoners led arriving prisoners to the lazaret to be executed; or wore armbands as part of the ruse at the lazaret; or cut the hair of the females to be executed; others played in the orchestra at the gate as part of that ruse, etc. Technically, this is assistance."

I sympathized with the judge's position, though I recalled from reading about the case and his earlier ruling that many considered him anti-Semitic. His conclusion seemed logical: any interpretation of the word "assistance" without taking into account whether it was voluntarily or involuntarily seemed to go against the grain of the word "assistance" as the framers of this legislation intended it to be read. Did they really want to put the US government in the position of seeking and then deporting those whose actions lacked the basic requisite of free will? That seemed inconceivable to me. Yet it also seemed that the judge did not have to go that far, to conclude that whether *involuntary* conduct, under duress, could not suffice to subject someone to being stripped of citizenship and deported. Here, By Fedorenko's own admission, his conduct was voluntary. In 1943 he had shot at Jews, a hundred or more, who managed to storm the camp's barbed-wire gates. (About a dozen did manage to escape and live to tell about it.) That act must have been *voluntary*. He was not stark-raving mad or deprived of food and water or clearly fearful for his life had he done otherwise than shoot at escaping Jews.

I remembered the famous passage I had studied in the Talmud as a youngster. If a man is threatened with death unless he kills another, the Talmud provides (Sanhedrin 74a): "Let him rather kill you, but you may not kill the other man. Who can say that your blood is redder than his?"

Clearly, Fedorenko's actions, in harming others in order to save his own life, found no defense in either the Talmud or US law.

But the most telling thing about Federenko's conduct that made it voluntary is that he had an opportunity to escape when accorded a biweekly four-hour furlough in the neighboring town. Of course, that was a highly risky proposition. But soldiers under field manuals, be they those of the US Army or of the Ukrainian or Red Army, are under an obligation to try to escape capture when accorded a reasonable opportunity, especially if not treated as a POW but impressed into service with the enemy.

The Justice Department could have filed an appeal on the narrow factual question of whether what we knew about Fedorenko's conduct placed it in the clearly "voluntary" category. But instead the Justice Department contended in a brief filed with the Fifth Circuit Court of Appeals that Federenko's concentration camp guard duty was inherently "assistance" whether voluntary or not. This seemed wrong to me. Why not show that his particular conduct *was* voluntary? Otherwise, the US citizenship of Jewish survivors who may have involuntarily "assisted," because it was in fact coerced, was at risk, resting on the slim reed of prosecutorial discretion.

On June 28, 1979, the US Court of Appeals for the Fifth Circuit issued its ruling. It noted that Fedorenko and all the other guards were given a four-hour furlough each week to a neighboring village and thus had an opportunity for attempting escape, thus giving the court ample opportunity to find that his particular conduct was indeed voluntary. But the Fifth Circuit chose instead to align itself with the Justice Department position that whether Fedorenko's behavior was voluntary or not was irrelevant. Beyond that, the Fifth Circuit formulated a new test: that it was sufficient, for purposes of denaturalization, that a US consular officer examining a visa application *might* have been led to undertake an investigation, which *might* have led to denial of a visa, had the applicant not provided misleading answers.

Reading that opinion gave me the chills. It seemed to open up the stripping of citizenship to a series of *"mights."* Fedorenko took his case to the Supreme Court, which, surprisingly, granted his petition for a writ of *certiorari*.

I started to sense that I was wading into turbulent waters. I did not want the US Supreme Court to uphold stripping citizenship on the narrowest of grounds, enabling deportation on that basis. The way out of this conundrum seemed to be asking the Supreme Court to do what the two courts below should have done: take Fedorenko's defense of involuntary conduct seriously, and then give the government an opportunity to prove that his conduct was indeed voluntary. Otherwise, what was the point of OSI? If we were not able to show that collaboration with the Nazis in facilitating the Holocaust was done by willing executioners—whether motivated by anti-Semitism or expediency— we were accomplishing no more than showing that the killers were no different than you or me, the average citizen, and casting these evil deeds in the glow of some moral equivalency, thus devaluing the whole point of accountability. If we were to ignore intent, what lesson, I wondered, were we imparting to future generations?

In addition to *Fedorenko*, I was also immersed in the *Osidach* case, and by my second week, Rockler instructed me to "go active" on that. He told me I'd be working with Bert Falbaum, an investigator from Treasury's Alcohol, Tobacco and Firearms Department, and that we'd be seeking depositions of potential witnesses.

"I want you to get rolling on that case with recommendations," Rockler said. "Okay?"

"Yes, sir. I'll make the arrangements. But one thing, if I may, on the *Fedorenko* case. I understand that main Justice will handle the response to the Supreme Court, but OSI will have a hand in it. I'd like to work on it and have us urge the Supreme Court to revert to a voluntary versus involuntary standard and examine each case on its facts."

"Look, Allan," Rockler said with an air that suggested little sympathy for my position. "The White House wants *strict enforcement of all immigration laws*. That means the Criminal Division is not going to take a position that allows illegal immigrants to clog the courts by saying, 'I didn't come here illegally, because I had no choice about what I did.'"

He turned toward me. "Besides Allan, it is a hell of a lot easier to ask the Supreme Court to simply affirm an appeals court decision than to ask it to pick and choose what's right and wrong about it and come up with some new formula. Don't get me wrong: I don't want Justice to ever go after Jews, kapos, orchestra musicians, or whatever. But that will never happen. Focus instead right now on nailing Osidach."

"Yes, sir," I said. But in fact I did not share his faith in the benevolence of prosecutorial discretion. Rockler's conviction that DOJ would never choose to prosecute Jewish survivors, even though they might technically have "assisted," was surely not something you could take to the bank. But I had my marching orders: focus on making the case against Osidach.

Before that, I needed to fly to Miami. It was time to talk to my parents. I had been putting it off for too long, choosing to keep them in the dark about my change in jobs until I met with them personally.

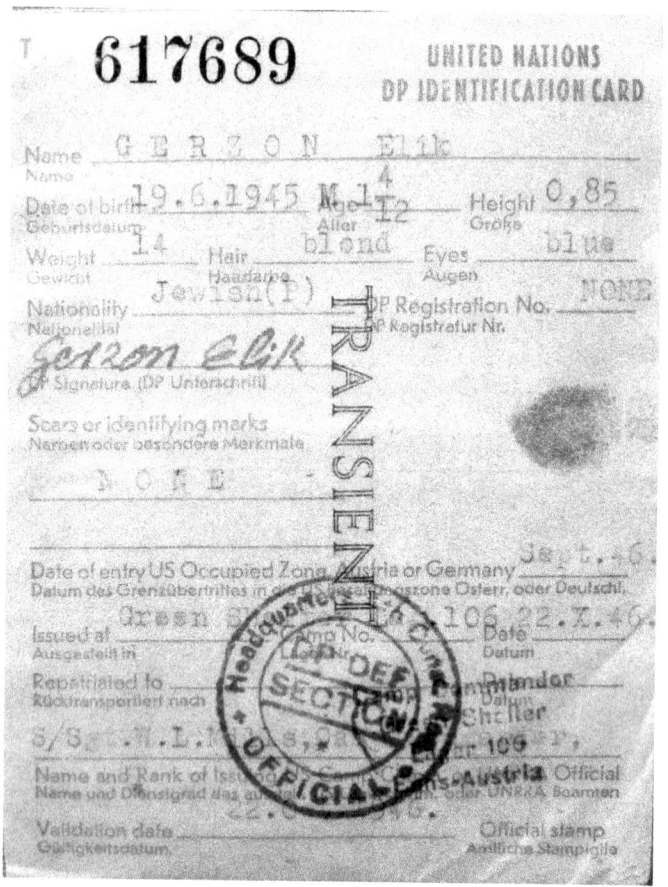

The Displaced Person identification and ration card for Allan Gerson, then known as Elik Gerzon.

Chapter Six

Surviving the War

The Soviet Union's deportation of Polish nationals has been treated as a historical footnote, but it deserves much greater attention. Estimates of the number deported vary, from 500,000 to 1.7 million, though the number of Jewish Polish deportees – about 200,000 – appears settled. The transfer of so many, in fetid, claustrophobic cars that chuffed across unimaginable distances (some treks were 2,500 miles), was a test of endurance and will.

My parents spent 14 days on their train to Siberia, before their car was left in a wooded settlement in the Ural Mountains. Russian guards drove about 30 captives 25 miles to a labor camp, surrounded by high white birch trees. It had several rotting barracks, where my parents shared one with the other six members of my father Mottel's family. A Russian commander and guards, who humiliated and disparaged the prisoners at every turn, ran the labor camp. Mottel knew Russian from his days in Kiev, so he could translate the commander's verbal barrages: "This will be your grave," the commander said. "Don't dream of going home. It will not exist anymore. There will never be a free Poland again."

Their beds were made of decrepit boards, with mice and rats as well as bedbugs scrambling about. (Some prisoners in other barracks tried to repel the bedbugs by placing the four corners of their bed in cups of water, but the insects climbed the walls to the ceilings and parachuted onto the bodies.) Their toilet was a hole in the middle of the bedroom. The Russians confiscated their clothes and made them wear rags. The captives' main objective was to stave off hunger, typhus, dysentery, and thoughts of suicide. Siberia had one redeeming quality. The air was so clean, my mother later said, she never got a headache.

Each morning they went to work. The men were driven an hour into the forest to cut trees for lumber. The Russians gave them daily quotas, but none of the prisoners had ever done such work. My father was a book keeper and his brother-in-law Shimon a peddler. Needless to say, they never met their goals. Nonetheless, each day for 12 hours, they chopped and cut and then returned to the barracks.

The women were no better equipped for their tasks. Walking a couple of miles to suitable grounds, they were given scythes and instructed to cut and bundle grass that could be fed to the horses in the coming winter.

The ordeal not only tested the prisoners' strength but, as Peshka discovered, their conscience as well.

Each morning the barracks was given a long chunk of bread, to be divided for eight people and eaten for lunch. Peshka volunteered to cut it—as a dressmaker, she took great pride in her precise cutting—so slicing water-logged bread provided odd comfort. She even used her measuring tape to ensure sixteen equal slices. One morning it occurred to her that if she cut seventeen equal pieces, she could keep one extra for herself, and no one would know. She did just that. But later that day, when she was in the fields and she opened her napkin for lunch, she saw the three pieces of bread… and started to cry. *What's happened to me*, she thought. *What's happened to me!* She tucked the three slices into the napkin, and when she reached the barracks in the evening, she put them on the table for all to see.

Peshka's sewing skills, beyond helping her cut bread, proved transformative.

She didn't mind hard labor, but she resented cutting tall grass with a steel blade that she barely knew how to hold. She told the commander, through Mottel, that she was an expert sewer and that she had her machine; perhaps instead of doing field work, she could mend the torn uniforms of the Red Army. The offer was accepted, and trucks soon began hauling in battered green jackets, pants, and overcoats. Peshka pulled out her machine and went to work. Various guards in the settlement noticed her craftsmanship, and they asked her to make dresses for their wives. Peshka's days in the field were over.

The summer weather was pleasant, but by late August, a deep

chill had arrived, soon bringing snow, ice, and fierce winds. Each day water was drawn from a well, but the water that splashed from the bucket created a dangerous slope of ice, and the frozen crankshaft could break and endanger its handler. Several thermometers were positioned around the camp. As long as the temperature was not less than 40 degrees below zero, the prisoners had to work. If the temperature was less than 40 degrees below zero, they got the day off.

At other labor camps, some of the captives received mail from relatives in Poland or Ukraine, which offered some clue about what was happening in their homelands. One letter said, "We envy you being in Siberia."

Peshka and Mottel knew little about events back home or in the war. They occasionally saw one of several Russian newspapers, but the government controlled them all. There was no radio or any passersby. Their only information came from what the Russians told them, which they didn't believe; the guards ensured their isolation. A town was within walking distance; Peshka wanted to go there and sell her dresses, but the Russians refused. In fact, they told all the prisoners there was no point trying to escape. They could go no farther than the next town, and the guards would track them down and kill them.

Peshka and Mottel survived the entire year; so, too, did everyone in their barracks. By October 1941, they were bracing for another winter when a Pole from nearby knocked on their door with news: "We are free."

On June 22, 1941, Germany invaded the Soviet Union in Hitler's largest single military operation of the war. Less than two years after the two countries had signed their non-aggression pact, the Germans deployed more than 3 million soldiers, supported by 650,000 troops from their allies, in an assault that stretched from the Baltic Sea in the north to the Black Sea in the south.

At the time, the Soviet Union had imprisoned about 2 million Polish citizens, including those they had deported. But after Germany's invasion, Stalin needed additional manpower, so in July, 1941 he reestablished diplomatic ties with Poland's government in exile, by then in London. The Sikorski-Mayski Agreement called for the release of all Polish prisoners held in Soviet camps, and those prisoners, along with other Poles, would form an army of 40,000 to fight under Soviet leaders in Russia and then under British commanders in Iran. Many of the Jews who had been imprisoned wanted to join, but most of them were rejected because the Polish authorities didn't want Jews in their military. There was one notable exception—Menachem Begin. During the war, he fought with the Polish army in Palestine and remained to lead the fight for Israel's independence, later becoming that country's prime minister.

Peshka and Mottel were eager to leave their labor camp in the Urals, but like all of the refugees, they had few options. They could not return home, as the West was closed because of the Soviet Union's war against Germany, and much of the East was closed due to preparations for war against Japan. That left a southern route, toward Iran, which could be a gateway to Palestine. It would also be someplace warmer. Peshka and Mottel, along with Mottel's family and others from their labor camp, boarded a railroad car. Sixteen months after they had arrived in Siberia, they headed south.

They were lucky. The Siberian labor camps were part of the Soviet Union's gulag and special settlement system that operated from the early 1920s to the 1960s. Made famous by Aleksandr Solzhenitsyn's "The Gulag Archipelago" (1973), the camps were always treacherous, but they were most deadly from 1941 to 1943, during the height of the war on the Eastern front. An estimated 516,000 inmates perished in the camps during those years, due to famine caused by the war and by increasingly harsh conditions. The Russians' anti-Semitism remained a permanent cudgel. The Polish Jews who were deported to Siberia in 1940 seemed doomed, but they won their freedom through events that they could have neither engineered nor imagined.

Beginning in the summer of 1941, hundreds of trains, now occupied by large numbers of Jewish-Polish refugees, traveled south, not only from Siberia but from wherever the Germans were encroaching. Most of the refugees did not have a specific destination in mind. Many dreamt of Palestine, but for now they were searching for a place with shelter, food, sanitation, and warm temperatures. As they traveled through Central Asia, along the once-important trade route known as the Silk Road, they encountered towns with dismal living conditions and outbreaks of typhoid, cholera, and other diseases. Almost by default, many of those on board these trains settled in Tashkent, the largest city in Uzbekistan, which was now part of the Soviet Union. But Tashkent's open sewers, crowded mud houses, and poverty forced the refugees to once again face extreme hardship and unforgiving scourges: malaria and typhoid claimed lives on a regular basis, filling cemeteries with tombstones inscribed with Hebrew.

Peshka and Mottel's railroad car was less oppressive than the cattle cars had been, as it had shelves on which to sleep, but the clustered, unclean environment still bred disease and discomfort. They reached Tashkent after 20 days, but the authorities turned them away, asserting that the city could not absorb any more migrants. The refugees traveled another 190 miles southeast to Samarkand, one of the oldest and most fabled cities in Central Asia, a center for Islamic study known for its splendid mosaic mosques.

Peshka and Mottel initially slept in a field but soon found a small apartment, and they tried to restart their lives. Their goal was to go to Palestine, but they took comfort for the time being in the sunshine and mild weather, as well as the fresh produce. They'd had no fruit in the Urals but here they had watermelons, peaches, and grapes. (Peshka later said when interviewed for the Spielberg Foundation project that, "they were the nicest grapes in the whole world.") However, the sheer quantity of the fruit caused some to gorge, their stomachs shrunken from malnutrition in Siberia, inducing dysentery and multiple deaths. Peshka pulled out her sewing machine to once again make dresses or to find any other sewing jobs, but she worked secretively. Corruption was rampant, and the refugees were most vulnerable to official abuse. To work legally, Peshka would have to buy a license and pay taxes that were higher than what she could earn. Instead, she sold her goods on the black market.

Mottel's sister, Chumah, and his brother-in-law, Moishe, were not so fortunate. They were arrested for selling items on the black market in a scheme that implicated the entire family. Moishe and Chumah, along with Mottel, bought cloth in large bolts and then cut them into smaller pieces to sell in the Central Bazaar of Samarkand. Chumah sat on their inventory, covering it up with a large flowing dress. After each piece was sold Moishe and Mottel came back to pick up another. But one day the police followed Moishe back to Chumah and both were arrested.

Russian prison during the war was a death sentence. When

there was not enough food for workers or the army why should the authorities allocate precious food to prisoners, parasites? Prisoners stayed alive in two ways: they received packages from their family or they stole packages from other prisoners. Moishe tried to protect his packages and he was soon murdered by prison gangs. Chumah heard him crying for help as he was beaten to death.

Desperate, she adopted a different strategy. She found the head of the toughest woman's gang and brought her the unopened packages she received form the family. The bargain was a simple exchange: keep me alive and I will keep giving you food I receive as gifts. The gang leader realized this meant giving Chumah some of the food to keep the packages coming.

Besides sending food, the family also tried to find a way to bribe Chumah out of prison. Many schemes went awry. In one, Mottel's younger brother, also named Moishe, found a prostitute that claimed to be sleeping with a prison official. She told Moishe that if he got her a new fancy dress she would use her charms to get Chumah released. The material was produced, the dress sewn by Peshka, but the story was fake.

Even the strongest and most violent women died in prison. Chumah expected that a tougher and more desperate prisoner would come along to challenge her protector. To survive she had to get released, and fast. She decided that the way out was through a Jewish doctor that had the authority to bring prisoners to the infirmary and, if he deemed necessary, release them for medical care outside.

All mail was heavily censored. So Norma wrote a letter that she met the doctor from Zamość, and that he was so poor that his shoes did not even have shoe laces. The family knew that the famous Jewish doctor died before the war and so this was code. They correctly surmised that Chumah was telling them in code that the prison doctor was Jewish and could be bribed. Mottel was the most articulate and business wise. He was also the oldest in the family and its leader. Mottel took the job of bribing the prison doctor on himself.

To try to win Chumah's release, Mottel needed money for bribes, so he found a job as a watchman at a site that collected grain from farms. But he only earned between 100 and 150 rubles a week ($1.50 to $2.25), which wasn't nearly enough to amass a decent bribe. Mottel therefore assumed his own risks. Peshka sewed him special underwear with deep pockets, used to stuff with grain, then smuggled home. He estimated that he could stuff 10 pounds of grain down each leg, plus a bit more around his abdomen. Mottel knew he was risking his life. One of Mottel's co-workers who lived near him also had inner linings sewn throughout his clothes. One day a lining sprung a leak and the authorities followed the trail of grain to his house. Mottel saw them coming and didn't know where the trail of grain ended, or who would be arrested. The neighbor was sentenced to seven years in prison, essentially a death sentence.

While Mottel amassed his money, the whole family agreed to contribute to the bribe. But how much was to be spent? It was during these extended deliberations that Peshka became exasperated at the attempt to logically work out the mathematics of the bribe for which her husband was risking his life and shouted, "How much? Everything, family is worth everything!"

The scheme worked; Chuma was released.

Peshka and Mottel still had little access to information beyond their immediate surroundings, and could not communicate with family or friends back home. They also remained in the dark about the war. But their fate was tied to events thousands of miles away.

After Japan attacked Pearl Harbor on December 7, 1941, the United States declared war against Japan. Germany and Italy, then declared war against the United States, which retaliated in kind. The American people had been deeply divided about Europe's latest conflagration, but now with their political leaders aligned, its industry mobilized, and the public in full support, the United States prepared for assaults in North Africa, Europe, and the Pacific.

The arrival of United States' military forces would not save the Jews in Europe. After Germany invaded Poland, it established ghettos to isolate and control the Jews. Those were followed by the SS and mobile death squad which were sent on killing rampages into German-controlled territories, targeting Jews and others. The Nazis began deporting thousands of civilians to new concentration camps, Auschwitz being the largest. By November, 1942, they had deported more than 100,000 people from the Zamość region. Hitler had begun to implement his Final Solution to the Jewish Question, the extermination of all Jews. By the end of 1942, Belzec, Treblinka, and Sobibor—as well as Auschwitz—were all operational, and all on Polish soil.

Peshka and Mottel had no hint of these developments until 1944, when a traveler passed through Samarkand. He told them that Zamość was *Judenrein,* or cleansed of Jews. It was unthinkable. The Jews had been in Zamość for hundreds of years.

Desperate for more information, Peshka wrote a letter to the mayor of Zamość and asked him what had happened to her parents. Weeks passed, and to her astonishment, the mayor responded: "What happened to your parents," he wrote, "is the same fate that befell all the Jews in Zamość."

By June, 1940, the Germans had begun sending the Jewish males in Zamość to labor camps. One group was sent to work at Belzec, about 30 miles south, and others to Izbica and Mokre and Labunie. The Jews who remained in Zamość were moved in April 1941 to an impoverished quarter in the New Town, in mostly dilapidated homes. About 7,000 Jews were hemmed into this ghetto, a diminishing number as the deportations to labor camps continued.

In March 1942, rumors began to circulate in the ghetto that the Germans were deporting Jews en masse to Belzec, 10,000 to 12,000 a day, and that they were now being killed "in a puzzling manner." Mieczyslaw Garfinkel, a lawyer in Zamość who was the chairman of the *Judenrat*, did not believe the reports, even after he had received confirmations of the gassings from eyewitnesses who had escaped.

On April 11, 1942, the deportations began, the ghetto in Zamość surrounded by the police and the SS, riding their horses, whips in hand. The Jews were assembled midday in the town square, where they waited without food or water until the evening. Those who were too old or ill or resistant were shot and killed in their houses or on the street. The others, about 3,000 of them, were forced onto trains headed for Belzec.

In his letter to Peshka, the mayor described nothing about what had actually happened, but he didn't have to. Both Peshka and Mottel knew that they would never again see their parents or their other loved ones who had stayed on in Zamość.

The war raged on, beyond the ken of Peshka and Mottel, who could only wait in a landlocked corner of Uzbekistan until the victors were determined.

Buoyed by the military strength of the United States, the Allies conquered Germany, which surrendered on May 7, 1945. Italy, after suffering defeats in the Balkans and North Africa, had signed an armistice with the Allies in 1943. Japan surrendered on August 15, 1945, after the United States dropped atomic bombs on Hiroshima and Nagasaki. Across the Axis powers, defeated governments were replaced, punished, or eradicated (Hitler shot himself in a bunker in April 1945); political boundaries were redrawn; territories were returned. And the full horrors of the Nazis slowly came to light. Auschwitz, Buchenwald, and Bergen-Belsen were all liberated in 1945, freeing tens of thousands of frail prisoners, but also giving outsiders their first view of industrialized carnage: the electric barbed wires and strategic watchtowers, the gas chambers that had suffocated three generations at a time, the shallow trenches of decomposed corpses that elevated the earth and emitted gases, the nearby farms that were fertilized with the ashes of the dead.

And there was Belzec, where in 1942 a half-million Jews were gassed in 10 months, where most of the Jews of Zamość were murdered, and where the chambers' double walls were effectively shut after no Jews were left within several hundred miles.

And then there were the displaced masses of the living. More than 50 million refugees dispersed across Europe and Asia—Germany alone had 11 million—which led to the largest population movement in European history. The Potsdam Conference in July 1945, with Great Britain, the Soviet Union, and the United States, sought to lay out the rules by which displaced persons could return to their homelands, and that included allowing the Polish Jews in Uzbekistan to return home.

After Peshka and Mottel learned that the war was over, they needed passports to return to Poland, which they could get through the Soviet authorities.

They experienced one other significant development. Their second son was born on June 19, 1945. The midwife said it looked like an "orange."

That orange was me.

Allan Gerson photographs his parents Paula and Morton Gerson, at their home in North Miami Beach, circa 1982.

Chapter Seven

Miami Chills

En route to Miami, to the first real conversation with my parents since taking the OSI job, I tried out lines that would explain my decision and why I had held off telling them about it for more than two weeks. At 34, I was still seeking parental approval.

But this was no ordinary job, and it went to the core of *their* being, *their* suffering. So I both hoped and expected that they would be thrilled with my announcement, view the new position as tied to divine justice, even though they didn't believe much in God. The reality, it occurred to me, was that they might believe my new venture could backfire into an *"andere falsche Got,"* another false God, as my father would often mutter under his breath when yet another hope was dashed by disappointment.

Though nearly three decades had passed since they reconstituted their lives in America, the past nevertheless gnawed mercilessly at them both. It could not be avenged. It could only be absorbed as a memory, by clinging to it like a hapless swimmer to a raft. They believed that the Holocaust had not merely turned the murdered Jews of Zamość into victims, but that somehow, their death rested on a higher plane. They were martyrs, and martyrs cried out to be honored.

Yet despite my reservations, I believed my parents would approve of, if not embrace, my new position. Could anyone have a stronger desire to see Nazi collaborators brought to justice? Could anyone have a greater stake in forcing the enablers to give up their reinvented American lives, to lose their United States citizenship, and to face deportation? And if that meant being dispatched to the Soviet Union to face a quickie trial for treason with a firing squad in its wake, so be it. My parents could surely live with that. The martyred deserved no less.

I realized that it might not be so easy for them, that other considerations might come into play. My parents had refrained from telling me many of the specifics about how they survived the war or how they made it to America, the part of their lives placed in my imaginary "Better Not To Know" box. This reticence was not uncommon among Holocaust survivors. Some memories are better left undisturbed.

They had been living for the past six months at Point East, a retirement community in North Miami Beach. It was pleasant enough, a reprieve from the harsh winters in the north and the burden of running a dry cleaning and tailoring establishment in the Bronx, which they had done for the previous 20 years. They had carefully saved their pennies, and when they saw their opportunity to move south, they seized it and had already made the adjustment. In no time, my father had become president of a new Jewish cultural center at their retirement enclave.

As I entered their condo, a warm sea breeze flowed through the open windows. My mother's hug was, as always, nearly overbearing. My father's approach was quite the opposite: a hand shake rendered without making eye contact. As Ma served her apple cake, I turned to explaining my mission.

"It's called OSI, the Office of Special Investigations, and it's a new part of the US Justice Department," I said. "The mandate is to track down Nazi collaborators who are living in America and to deport them." Then, beaming, I drew from my pocket my new badge and my Justice Department ID card, which included my headshot.

But instead of visible pride, a curtain of dead silence descended. My mother's face hardened as my father's gaze sunk.

Perhaps they were waiting for some elaboration, so I began again. "What the badge signifies," I said, "is that you're looking at OSI's first trial attorney." But the only look I got from my mother, still beautiful after all these years, was one of consternation, as if I had just announced my intention to abandon the practice of law in favor of becoming a professional thug.

My father's face remained blank, his eyes still averting my gaze as his fingers stayed busy nudging with his fork the last bit of pastry.

He looked up, breaking the icy silence. "My son, I don't know if this is really good for you," he said, peering into the distance through his thick farsighted lenses. "You were doing so well at your job."

That was true, at least by all outward appearances. While at DOJ's Civil Division, I had argued cases all over the country, most of them successfully. My salary was sufficient to keep Joan and Daniela, then a two-year-old charmer, warm and fed. But I desired something on a grander scale, something tied to promoting fundamental human rights, if not making a difference in matters of war and peace. At OSI I had the opportunity to make sure that the bad guys who were living the good life here in America wouldn't win in the end. *Didn't he get that*?

Besides, although I had resisted the idea that my family history should be a driving factor in my work at OSI, the fact is that once I became immersed in the work, reading the files and visualizing the accounts of the death camps, I recognized that I was indeed now in a position to in some small way avenge my parents' suffering and my family's deaths.

But this calculus didn't seem to be getting across. My parents continued to seem uneasy, which only befuddled me more and more as we fell into an awkward silence.

I looked around the room. The balcony door was open, the sun bathing the living room in a soft glow. I had seen their Florida place once before, several months earlier, when I helped them settle in. Their condo had since become a hybrid of Miami tropical with Bronx stolid decor: a new white sofa and chairs squared off against the dark mahogany credenza and oversized cocktail table that they had brought from their residence up north. The marriage of styles captured the past and present of my parents' lives in America.

I knew it wasn't good asking my father directly why he wasn't happy. He would always say when such questions were asked: "*if man darf schoen fragen, ist schoen garnicts veg*," if one has to ask, it's already worthless. But I nudged him on to reveal what it was about my new job that was bugging him.

"Because what you're after was a long time ago. The Nazis are already dead."

"Not all of them, Dad, and not their helpers."

"And you're the one who's going to catch these people and deport them? As if this is your destiny?"

I explained to him that we were not going to be trying them for war crimes in the death camps and elsewhere, but that we were pursuing the collaborators on visa fraud. When they applied for US visas, they swore that they had never assisted in persecution, but that's what they did. So, their visas are invalid because they were based on lies. As a result, their US citizenship can be revoked.

"Then," I concluded, "we can then get rid of them."

"You mean, deported?" he said

"Yes, precisely."

That was hardly assuring. *"Herzach si, mein son,"* Listen here, my son, he said after pausing for a long moment, as if to measure his words. "So many people lied back then. It wasn't so easy to get into America after the war, when the quota for Jews lightened a bit and then tightened. You had to have a relative as a sponsor. And a job waiting for you in an occupation considered in demand. Do you remember our friend David?"

"Of course, in New York."

"Yes, David, who had tuberculosis, swore when the Americans interviewed him that he was healthier than a cow. And Joseph, who lives next door to us now." Dad pointed out the window to the neighboring condo. "Joseph claimed he was a carpenter, and the fact is, he doesn't know a hammer from a sickle."

He paused, and then said slowly, quietly, "And don't forget our own not-so-straight path to becoming citizens here, the risks we took, what we endured."

I realize what my father was getting at; that we too might be in jeopardy. Or if not us directly, perhaps my Uncle Henik, for he had survived Auschwitz. But how?

"I'm trying to understand. What are you getting at, Dad?" I said as I took up my teacup to steady myself against a growing agitation.

I fell back on the nuances of the law. "OSI won't be concerned about white lies Jewish survivors made," I said, thinking I had gotten to the source of his concerns.

"What is 'a white lie?'"

"It's one that isn't a crucial misrepresentation; it's not a lie like claiming you weren't a guard at a death camp or saying you didn't round up the Jews to send them to their death when you did. The ones that did that, who voluntarily chose to help the Nazis, they're the ones, the only ones, we are after."

But I had managed only a dent in his universe of concern. "That's still a wide net that could catch many Jews."

"Please," I said. "OSI's only purpose is to go after Nazi collaborators living in America. It's about those who had a choice, and they chose to help Hitler."

My mother sat back on the couch. Crossing her legs, she placed a napkin over her knees. Her own plate of strudel remained untouched. Her silence hung heavily over every word of my give-and-take with Dad.

"So technically, if I understand correctly, although I am of course not a lawyer like you," Dad said, determined to make his point, "OSI will be taking away their citizenship not because of what they did, the atrocities they committed, but because they lied about it. It's a little like getting Al Capone for tax evasion, no?"

"No, Dad. Putting Al Capone on trial for tax evasion didn't shed any further light on organized crime. It was simply a way of putting him away in prison."

"So how is OSI different?" he asked

I placed my cup of tea on the table. "Don't you see? It's the opposite. We put these collaborators on trial for immigration fraud, and during the course of that trial we will shed light on the role they, and collaboration generally, played in perpetration of the Holocaust."

"So, it will be about the Holocaust?" my father asked.

"Yes, of course!" I replied, perhaps too readily. I sought out my father's eyes. "It'll be about the Holocaust itself. How it was perpetrated. Who the willing helpers were, how the collaborators made it possible."

"*Oy Gottenu*, Oh, my God, have mercy," Ma suddenly uttered, breaking her silence with a deep sigh.

"So now why all of sudden this new push?" she asked. "All these years and the government never cared about these people before. So why is the US government now in such a big hurry?"

She sat upright, staring at me as if I were on trial. "Haven't you moved around enough? You have degrees galore. You don't want to lay down roots? You have to settle down."

I folded my arms into a self-protective barrier. "Look, Congress has had a number of reports of Nazi collaborators living undisturbed in America."

"So?" Ma sighed again. I could see her thinking that I was walking into this blindly, chasing ghosts, leaving prudence by the wayside. "You think we don't know that?"

She held her arms out from her sides, as if closing in on her summation. "But what about your future? Where is your future in this?"

I stood my ground. "Look. I want to do this because it's important. I thought you—you and Dad, more than anyone—would understand that."

My mother burrowed her fork into a piece of strudel. "If it's so important, let others do it! You are not made for this kind of work." That hurt. Did she think I was too soft?

Dad joined in, his voice calm but resolute. "Maybe your mother is right. Maybe you should let others do it."

What could be going through their minds? It was one thing to repeatedly proclaim "never forgive, never forget"; quite another to have their son go into the maelstrom, confront these tormentors, the embodiment of the beast that had engulfed their lives in such untold misery. What parent wouldn't want to spare their child from re-experiencing their torment, and at the price of passing on an otherwise sensible career? Then this thought occurred to me: perhaps there was unspoken matter that they didn't want to touch upon.

I pushed those thoughts aside. Our conversation had reached an impasse. There was nothing I could do to relieve their anxiety.

"Dad, I've made my decision," I said, as I stood up. "I respect everything you and Ma have said, I really do, but I have to follow my instincts. Please don't worry. I assure you that it will all work out for the best."

"*Allevai*, It should only be so," Ma said. She hugged me, and Dad patted me on the back as if to say, I am proud of you, regardless of what you do.

My whirlwind visit had spiraled in ways I hadn't anticipated. As I headed to the rental car for the trip back to the airport, I gave them one last look. They stood on the balcony overhead, waving a cheerless goodbye. I waved back.

At Foehrenwald Displaced Persons Camp many of the refugees had children, including Peshka and Mottel. Peshka, second from left, holds baby Sam and Allan leans on her.

Chapter Eight

The Remnant

Tens of thousands of Polish Jews had been deported deep into the Soviet Union, but now after the war, they had to embark home on rambling trains. The trip from Uzbekistan to Poland, passing through Moscow, was well over 2,500 miles, and meant a return to a land of ruin, although Zamość and other small towns had escaped physical desolation. Still, it was a terrain dotted by the smokestacks of death camps and haunted by memory. Before the Second World War, 3.3 million Jews had lived in Poland. By war's end, only 300,000 had survived, and 80 percent of those had been saved by their deportation to the Soviet Union.

Those Jews expected to return home so they could rebuild their lives. But when they crossed the Polish border, the local Poles seemed surprised that any Jews had survived, and they made clear that the Jews were not wanted. Their trains were met with anti-Semitic signs and banners, with one reading: "For every carload of coal we get from the Russians, we get a carload of Jews." The documentary "Saved by Deportation" interviewed seven deported Jews who were on these trains, and several of them described the murderous tactics of Polish militiamen, who boarded the cars and forced the male passengers to drop their pants to affirm that those they were readying to shoot were indeed Jews.

As Rudolf Weiss recalled, "We did not expect the trail left by the Nazis to be so ingrained in the country."

My parents left Samarkand, with me in tow, in the summer of 1946, well after the end of the war. Mindful of the risks, they might have waited to travel until I was at least a year old. I have no memory of that trip, but I do wonder if it somehow logged into my subconscious. Whether it is recorded there or not, it has become part of my collective memory of stories passed down by my parents. More an impression than a memory, to this day I have a warm, fuzzy feeling of dimly lit trains making long journeys through the night.

Even though they knew their families had all been exterminated, my parents wanted to return to Zamość, that remained for them their beloved ancestral home. But when they passed the Polish border, they heard what had just happened to the Jews in Kielce.

Located in south central Poland, Kielce had been depopulated of all Jews during the war, but about 200 had returned by 1946. In July, a non-Jewish man reported that his nine-year-old boy was missing. After the boy returned, the child told the police that he had been held captive at a large building used to shelter Jewish residents and several Jewish institutions. The boy's allegation tapped into an ancient myth of Jews using the blood of Christian children for their rituals. The authorities sent soldiers to the Jewish building, and a confrontation ensued, with each side suffering casualties. A mob then descended upon the Jews, with steelworkers, farmers, and other townsmen using guns, bayonets, and stones. At least 42 Jews were killed and more than four were wounded, including women and children. Many years later, the boy who had made the initial charge would acknowledge that he had never been abducted. But at the time, the pogrom in Kielce, combined with other attacks against Jews in Poland, spurred a Jewish exodus from the country.

My parents were part of that exodus, vowing never again to set foot on Polish soil. They jumped off their train with me and their meager possessions, deciding to reverse course and head south. After seven years and thousands of miles of wandering from Poland to Siberia to Uzbekistan and back to Poland, they were stateless, part of the displaced millions of post-war Europe. They buried their dream of returning to Zamość. They assumed someone else was already living in their home. Let them have it.

The Allies recognized the emergent humanitarian disaster of displaced masses, even before the war was over. In 1943, a 44-nation conference at the White House led to the creation of the United Nations Relief and Rehabilitation Administration (UNRRA). It had several purposes, including the assistance of refugees after the war; in 1945, immediately upon Germany's surrender, it began opening Displaced Persons (DP) camps in Germany, Italy, and Austria. But the camps failed miserably. For months, many survivors remained behind barbed wire, under armed guards, malnourished, sometimes even wearing the striped pajamas given to them by the Nazis. Thousands died from disease and malnutrition.

With even the victorious countries in ruins, UNRRA could not have anticipated the full scope of the crisis it had inherited, but its failure was also the result of the contempt held for Jews, especially the survivors, by one of America's most canonized generals.

In June 1945, General George S. Patton was assigned responsibility for United States' DP operations. The headstrong, controversial commander who led military campaigns in the Mediterranean, across France and into Germany wanted to be reassigned to the Pacific, where the fighting continued. But he was appointed military governor of Bavaria and overseer of the DP camps. His primary concern, however, appeared to be not giving offense to Germany, which he saw as a future ally to the United States. He also had a habit of downplaying Nazi atrocities, which hinted at the rank anti-Semitism that later emerged in his diaries.

General Patton referred to the displaced Jews as "sub-human" and "lower than animals," and at one DP camp, he entered a makeshift synagogue on Yom Kippur and wrote that it "was packed with the greatest stinking mass of humanity I have ever seen. Of course, I have seen them since the beginning and marveled that beings alleged to be made in the form of God can look the way they do or act the way they act."

Under General Patton, the DP camps intermingled Jews with Nazis, often behind barbed wire, sometimes in barely reconstituted former German concentration camps like Bergen-Belsen. The Jewish refugees—the "*Sh'erith ha-Pletah*," "the surviving remnant," as they referred to themselves—clamored for DP camps of their own.

Faced with complaints by Jewish groups, President Harry Truman sent Earl Harrison, the dean of the University of Pennsylvania Law School and an active member of various human rights organizations concerned with the plight of the refugees, to investigate. He returned with an unsparing report in August 1945. "As matters now stand," he wrote, "we appear to be treating the Jews as the Nazis treated them except that we do not exterminate them. They are in concentration camps in large numbers under our military guard instead of SS troops. One is led to wonder whether the German people, seeing this, are not supposing that we are following or at least condoning Nazi policy."

Harrison urged the creation of separate camps for Jews and other nationalities. It was imperative, he wrote, that the Jewish remnant have camps of their own if America was not to fall short of its promise to do all it can to enable the survivors of the Holocaust to live out their lives in dignity.

His recommendations were opposed not only by General Patton but also by Great Britain, which worried that separate camps would spur Jewish nationalism and calls for a Jewish state in Palestine, which was then under Great Britain's control. But President Truman, moved by Harrison's appeal, ordered General Dwight D. Eisenhower, the supreme allied commander, to implement the proposals. The first step: relieving General Patton of his military governorship in August 1945. (General Patton died later that year in a car accident in Germany.)

The conditions of the DP camps gradually improved, and they also increased in number. By 1946, nearly 300 were in operation, with 250 administered by the U.S. military.

Stateless, my parents once again considered Palestine. Other Jewish refugees were trying to immigrate there, but my parents knew it was already like a war zone and would be difficult to reach with a young child. They thought the U.S. was a possibility, but they would have to reach an American zone in Europe. Still traveling with my father's siblings and their spouses, they made it to Legnica, in southwest Poland, and then continued about 300 miles south, through Czechoslovakia and past the Austrian border to a DP camp, Gerestreet, in the British zone of occupation, near Linz. The sprawling complex had more than 150,000 Jews pass through it in the first five years after the war.

I have no memory of Linz, but I have two photographs of my parents from around that time. I assume both were taken at refugee processing centers. My mother's skin is surprisingly unblemished, the high cheekbones the same, the space between her front two teeth still visible. But the image is stark and raw: she has a thousand-mile stare. My father doesn't look nearly as worn as my mother, his eyes still firm and steady. Perhaps he suffered less or found other ways to carry the burdens.

As my parents described it, they and their traveling group were told in 1948 that living conditions were better in a camp called Foehrenwald, southwest of Munich in the American zone of occupation. Movement was not that easy between camps, but they had their ways honed in years of travel and so we traveled about 170 miles west into Germany to our new home.

The buildings at Foehrenwald had been constructed in 1939 for employees of the vast IG Farben chemical company, which profited from nearby slave labor camps. The site became a DP camp in June 1945. The authorities were nothing if not resourceful in repurposing venues of evil: The biggest DP camp, Landsberg, also near Munich, was on the site of a former concentration camp; the next-biggest DP camp, Feldafing, was originally a summer camp for Hitler Youth, and before that a fancy vacation spot where my wife Joan's paternal family from nearby Augsburg, frequented in the summers before emigrating to the United States before WW II. Foehrenwald was the third largest.

Foehrenwald's industrial roots meant that it had superior housing compared to that in other camps, with sturdy, heated homes; it also had its own police department, fire fighters, disciplinary commission, post office, and hospital. At its peak, Foehrenwald had more than 5,000 residents.

My earliest memories are from there, splashing in puddles with my cousin Sol — Aunt Chumah's firstborn who was born only a month apart from me in Uzbekistan — and roaming the outskirts of the pristine white birch forest surrounding the camp. I also had a dog, Blacky, a retriever who followed me wherever I went.

One day, my father and I rode into the neighboring town of Wolfratshausen on his creaky old motorbike. En route, the bike hit a rut and overturned, causing a cut above my right knee where a slight scar remains. In Wolfratshausen, I fixated on stores with meager goods for sale, many canned, but which nearly always managed to be neatly aligned or arranged in pyramid style making these sparse items appear not shabby but almost as works of art in their own right.

My father found work with the camp's Joint Distribution Committee (JDC), an American organization that was created in 1914 to help Jews in Central and Eastern Europe, which assisted UNRRA and the US military in running the DP camps after the war. My father, drawing on his bookkeeping experience, was named the deputy of the JDC in November of 1950, a position that put him at the nerve center of the camp.

My mother worked as a seamstress, but she had more important matters to tend to. She gave birth to my brother Sam on April 21, 1948, and he became part of a Displaced Person diaper brigade. My mother was among 200 women who were pregnant at Foehrenwald, and the fruition of those pregnancies on German soil was all the more exquisite. In the failed aftermath of the Third Reich, the survivors multiplied.

They also married. Aunt Ruchsa, who had been widowed since her husband Moishe's death in a Soviet prison outside Samarkand, found her second life partner at Foehrenwald. Her husband, Henik, was one of the most memorable figures of my youth. He was short and built like a brick, always with a cigarette stub in his hand, a gravel voice, and an attitude that fused self-assurance with menace. I knew as a child that he had lost his wife and three children in some mean place named *Oy-chwitz* (that's how they pronounced it), where he survived for three years and weighed less than 100 pounds when he was liberated. He always muttered under his breath, "*Yavol, Yavol,*" the guttural "Yes, sir" used to address his German enslavers. He mocked them at Auschwitz even as he followed their orders, and he responded to authority that way for the rest of his life.

He also wore a gold Patek Phillipe watch on his left wrist, an inexplicable accessory that added to his mystique. One day I told him how pretty it looked, and he invited me into his small hut, along a row of houses that looked like military barracks, where he proceeded to show me two more equally resplendent timepieces with the proud exclamation: "*amesdeke* Pateks," or true Pateks.

How did he get them? Even as a boy, I could sense the strange juxtaposition of the elegant watch on his wrist against the number tattooed in dark, sickly blue ink on his forearm. The digits began with the numeral 3, signifying that he was among the first groups deported to Auschwitz in 1942, and thus the least likely group to persevere until liberation. His survival was something of a mystery. Did his fireplug build give him some physiological capacity to endure or a reduced need for nourishment? Or could it be, as some whispered, that his durability was related to the *Pateks*—that he herded fellow prisoners in exchange for rewards or privileges? No one knew.

All I knew was that he was a warrior, a fact that he would sometimes lord over my parents. Once, he snapped at them as they were recalling their experiences in Siberia. "You don't know nothing!" he yelled. "You don't know about the dogs!" The death camp had vicious dogs, he told us, that could quickly rip a grown man to shreds. Uncle Henik once unexpectedly turned my palms upward and pronounced: "You would have never survived! You have no calluses! Right away to the gas chambers."

Years later, I would read *Survival at Auschwitz*, in which its Italian author Primo Levi recalls reaching for an icicle outside his window to satisfy his great thirst. Instantly, a camp guard tore it away.

"*Warum?*" Why? Levi asked.

The guard abruptly brought him to his senses. "*Hier ist kein warum!*" Here there is no why.

My parents had been deported to Siberia, where some semblance of rationality, even civility, prevailed alongside the cruelty, and indeed they resisted the designation of Holocaust survivor because they had never been interned in a death camp.

Uncle Henik was different. He survived the land of "*kein warums.*"

The DP camps were not permanent. We had to go somewhere. We all had to. One option remained Palestine. Haganah, the Zionist military organization, urged Europe's Jewish refugees to move there, and Uncle Moishe and Aunt Rushka did that in 1947. Members of Haganah pleaded with my parents as well, including in 1947, when the United Nations announced a partition plan for Palestine that would create independent Arab and Jewish states. Israel declared itself an independent state in 1948, followed by an armistice agreement the following year with the invading Arab states. My parents felt a deep connection to the new Jewish state, but reaching it at the time was treacherous, and Israel remained surrounded by enemies. My parents had also received a letter from friends in Israel, which said that the difficult conditions bred terrible diseases for infants, and that was enough to deter my mother. Even without children, she might have refused to go. She was a refined woman who, unless forced, wanted no part of the rough edges of civilization. She would often say that if she had ever been put in a concentration camp, she would have immediately run for the wires. She had, she told my father, suffered enough. She wasn't about to bring her two young sons or herself into a new, underdeveloped state still fighting for its survival.

The other travel option was the United States, which posed its own challenges. In 1945, President Truman recognized Europe's refugee crisis and, facing Congressional inaction, issued an executive order that gave immigration preference to displaced persons. Over the next three years, between 35,000 and 40,000 DPs, most of them Jewish, entered the U.S. But that number was still a fraction of the estimated 250,000 Jewish DPs in Europe. In 1948, President Truman again pushed for a more liberal immigration policy, and Congress passed the Displaced Persons Act. It authorized the entrance of 200,000 displaced persons to the US, but it restricted eligibility to people who had entered Germany, Austria, or Italy before December 22, 1945—thus discriminating against Jews, many of whom, including my parents, had been in Soviet-controlled territories until after that date. President Truman criticized the bill but signed it anyway.

With so few visas available, my parents could only bide their time in Foehrenwald. Obtaining entry was much easier if you had a relative in the U.S. who could sponsor you, and my dad had a rich second cousin on Long Island. But he had failed to pay his taxes and was in trouble with the law, so he couldn't help us. Then in 1950, Congress amended the Displaced Persons Act, increasing the quotas and removing the restrictions on geography and time. Foehrenwald's numbers began to dwindle, and the departures included my cousin Sol and his parents to America in 1949.

My own family would eventually leave as well. In November 1950, we were still in Foehrenwald, and there is a photograph of my parents and me along with Uncle Henik and Aunt Ruchsa. What's striking is that the fear appears gone from their eyes; they brim with hope. My mother, dressed in a long coat and neatly coiffed, rests her elegantly gloved hand reassuringly on my shoulder. I am attired in a three-piece suit that she fashioned for me, replete with tie and pocket square. Dad looks confident through his thick glasses. Uncle Henik has the stub of a cigarette in his fingers, but he is relaxed. To his right is Aunt Ruchsa, and she too rests her hands on my shoulder.

Perhaps they looked hopeful because the very next month we'd all be leaving Foehrenwald. Nothing in the photograph suggests the plot that my parents had hatched to win our departure, a plot that carried extraordinary risk. Despite more liberal immigration laws, gaining entry into the US was still difficult. Quotas still applied. Ukrainians, for example, could come in under more favorable terms accorded to farmers, but Jewish farmers were scarce. Most were urban tradesmen, unfavored by immigration restrictions. My parents had neither a valued occupation nor proof of a sponsor or relative who could help them gain entry.

Was it courage or foolhardiness that propelled them to take this next step on their journey?

I would not learn any of the details for many years. All I knew was that the next month, we traveled 470 miles north to the embarkation point of Bremerhaven, and on December 10, 1950, we boarded the *USNS General C.C. Ballou*. At 523 feet in length and 12,666 gross tons, it had been used previously to ship troops to Marseille. Now it had more than 1,000 passengers on board, including many Jewish refugees from Eastern Europe…the remnant…and yet the passengers also surely included some of those who had collaborated with the Nazis, either as concentration camp guards, police chiefs, or disseminators of hate. They were on the same ship we were, all jostled together in common purpose, all willing to leave the past behind. As we drifted down the Wesner River toward the North Sea and then to the Atlantic, plowing through the waters at 17 knots, I can only imagine the emotions of my parents as they stood on the deck and watched the Europe that had been their homeland fade into the distance.

It was winter. The high waves and the blustery cold put us all in a chill, and everything was gray. The men and women slept in separate quarters, but families congregated on deck during the day. Displaced Person transports were later called "Cargoes of Hope" or "Ships to Freedom," and between 1948 and 1952, they carried an estimated 80,000 Jewish DPs to the United States. But these were not easy trips, and those who died on board were buried at sea, with passengers gathered at the rail to offer final prayers.

Our voyage lasted eleven days, and as our ship entered New York Harbor, seagulls swooped about, and I extended my arm and tilted my hand to block the skyline. I proudly told my dad: *"Tata, New York ist nicht azoi gross. Ich kennen dekn es met meyn kleine hant!"* ("Daddy, New York is not that big. I can cover it with my small hand!")

The *Ballou* continued its humanitarian mission of shipping European refugees for two more years, until it was redirected across the seas and began carrying US troops to Korea.

Allan Gerson, with dog Blackie, at Fohrenwald Displaced Persons Camp.

Chapter Nine

A Calculus of Evil

In my early months at OSI, I realized I had different objectives from those of my colleagues. As someone who had no criminal law experience, I was always a bit of an outlier—it really wasn't my temperament to go for the jugular. But temperament alone wasn't the issue. What distanced me from the others was our view of the mission, a divide made clear to me during a deposition of a prominent Romanian rabbi.

Moses Rosen was the chief rabbi of Romania who was also a deputy in the parliament. In 1940, as the leader of a small synagogue, he was arrested and deported to a detention camp by the Iron Guard, a paramilitary force that looted, terrorized, and killed Jews. Rosen was released after several months, when the Iron Guard lost power in the government, but the attacks on Romania's Jewish community had only begun. The country's fascist government entered the war as an ally of Nazi Germany, and Romanian troops persecuted or massacred unthinkable numbers of their Jewish countrymen: One half of the 800,000 Jews who lived in Romania before the war died in the Holocaust. The others, including Rosen, survived by going into hiding. They could only return to their lives after a coup overthrew the government in 1944.

We believed that Rosen could help us gather information on a controversial American archbishop, Valerian Trifa. Before and during the war, Trifa had been one of the leaders of the Iron Guard who had rallied support for Hitler. Trifa immigrated to the United States in 1950, was ordained as a bishop in the Romanian Orthodox Church, and became a U.S. citizen. He was also a source of great public outcry—an important religious figure to some, a "Nazi terrorist," as he was called in the press, to others.

Rabbi Rosen had supposedly witnessed Trifa organize pogroms against the Jews, so OSI brought him to the United States for a deposition in June 1979. I wasn't directly involved in the case, but I was asked by Marty Mendelsohn, who was then still acting as Rockler's deputy, to depose the rabbi. I had never done a deposition before, but that seemed of little import as I had read enough transcripts of depositions, so it hardly seemed beyond my ken. Besides, I wanted to meet Rabbi Rosen. For me it was like meeting Rockler for the first time: touching history.

We met in OSI's offices along with a lawyer for Trifa, George E. Woods, who had been the US Attorney for the Eastern District of Michigan from 1953 to 1960. (Trifa himself did not attend.) With me from OSI was only a young intern, Eli Rosenbaum, a third-year student at Harvard Law School, who would in 1988 be appointed as OSI's third director. Rosen was 67, short, and rotund, with a white beard and sunken eyes. He was revered by Romanian Jews, who referred to him as "His Eminence," a spiritual leader who embodied the resistance and resolve of that community. As we sat around a table before the deposition began, and before Woods arrived, I decided to do something unusual; speak to Rosen in Yiddish to, as I put it in my diary for that day, "put him at ease." Soon, Woods arrived, wearing patent leather shoes and pants with a heavy buckle, and our short foray into Yiddish came to an abrupt end. It wouldn't take long to discover that Woods could be very nasty on cross-examination.

My aim was simple: to elicit from Rosen what he observed or knew about Trifa's persecution of the Jews. We needed precise answers to narrow questions about those actions, as Trifa's failure to disclose them could subject him to charges of immigration fraud. True, I wanted something more than that. I wanted to hear Rosen's whole story—what happened to the Jews of Romania, who was responsible for their deaths, how did the survivors survive, what role did the country's other institutions—religious, political, business—play in the Holocaust?

In short, I wanted to learn from Rabbi Rosen the complex, tragic narrative of what had happened to the Jews of Romania. But I knew that OSI would not want me to stray far off target and that Trifa's lawyer would vehemently object at every step of the way. I confined my questioning to concise descriptions that left as little room for challenge as possible.

Woods would later claim that Bishop Trifa was simply "critical of what he and so many others felt was undue influence of Romanian Jews in the political and economic fabric." On November 1, 1983, President Reagan would appoint him to a seat on the US District Court for the Eastern District of Michigan.

That night I began to wonder if this assignment was getting too personal for me. In my diary, I wrote, "The magnitude of this is dawning on me. The Holocaust is not only the central experience of this century but all centuries." I also noted that "the Holocaust is not possible as a German solo act."

Trifa went on trial for immigration fraud in 1982, but on its third day, he agreed to settle the case, acknowledging that he had been a member of the Iron Guard and had concealed that fact upon entering the United States. He agreed to leave the country on his own and immigrated to Portugal, where he remained until his death in 1987.

The outcome was hailed as a major victory for OSI. This was our mission—to deport Nazi collaborators—and if they were widely known, all the better. But even in that initial deposition, I felt that our pursuit of justice against any one suspect, notorious or not, had to be tied to exposing this larger truth of the Holocaust.

I never saw Rabbi Rosen again. After his deposition, he returned to his homeland and remained one of the most important figures in world Jewry until his death in 1994.

My primary assignment centered on Wolodymir Osidach, the former police chief of Rawa-Ruska who was living in Philadelphia. We had eyewitnesses who confirmed that during the war years, that was indeed his job, but we were seeking a witness who could specifically testify that Osidach had been involved in rounding up and deporting Jews to Belzec. That took me to Los Angeles in the fall of 1979, and to a meeting with Jaroslaw Sarowycz [not his real name], who had been a liaison between the SS and Osidach.

I arrived late at Los Angeles International Airport, where I was met by Bertram Falbaum, or Bert, as everyone at OSI affectionately called him. He had flown in from Washington. As nearly always, he had an unfiltered Chesterfield dangling from his lips as he stood waiting for me at the passengers' arrival gate. He asked about my trip and said that under ordinary circumstances, he would suggest we stop for drinks; but we had a big day ahead of us tomorrow, and he suggested instead that we simply pick up our rental car and head straight to our hotel. I was dead-tired and happily agreed with his suggestion.

As a criminal investigator, Bert carried a firearm, though we did not believe that the subjects of our investigation were dangerous (with the exception of Andrija Artukovic, a former minister of justice of the Nazi puppet state of Croatia). But both Sarowycz and Osidach were long-time members of the Organization of Ukrainian Nationalists (OUN), and there was no telling what extreme measures that close-knit organization might take.

Bert had already interviewed Sarowycz once, with another criminal investigator who was in the area, Tom Fusey. During that visit, Bert was able to secure Sarowycz's identification of Osidach as the police chief, but no more information was forthcoming, nor was any more expected. Investigators, like FBI agents, report to the Justice Department attorneys who are supervising the case and who are responsible for the ultimate determination on whether to use a particular witness. In this instance, we needed Sarowycz to turn on his fellow Ukrainian by describing Osidach's role in the liquidation of Rawa-Ruska's Jews. That was not the job of an investigator but was the job of one of the lead attorneys, which made it my job.

We knew that during the war, Sarowycz had been a translator for the SS, and thus he "assisted" the murderers. But we had no precedent for denaturalizing an individual for this type of "assistance" in persecution. Our best hope was that Sarowycz would cooperate with us, but I had to convey the potential serious (although maybe unenforceable) consequences against him if he failed to do so.

Sarowycz lived in Buena Park, about 20 miles southeast of Los Angeles, and while we drove there, I felt a nervous lump in my stomach. I was glad that Bert was with me. He was short and squat and 12 years my senior, but he looked 20 years older. Maybe it was the cigarettes, two packs a day, and the smoker's cough, much like Rockler's. Maybe his time in the service had aged him as well. He had enlisted in the Air Force at 17, was trained as a radio technician, and was sent off to the Korean War. Placed on a small Japanese island, he monitored all communications along the hotly contested 38th Parallel, and he remained in Asia for five more years after the war ended as part of America's deployment to maintain the status quo.

Upon returning to the States, his surveillance skills served him well, as he worked for the Treasury Department: first as a Customs official and then as deputy chief of law enforcement at the Fish and Wildlife Service. He retired from that office in 1979 to join OSI as its first criminal investigator, and we quickly bonded. His understated humor was appealing, but so too his professionalism and experience. Nothing rattled him, which was reassuring when you're about to meet someone who played a role, however tangential, in the murder of 18,000 Jews.

We approached a row of sleepy cottages, and Bert rounded the corner close to Sarowycz's house, where a neatly tended garden could be seen beyond a white wooden fence. Bringing the car to a stop, Bert looked things over and then asked, "Okay if I do one more time around the block? Just need to case the joint to see if there are any out-of-state license plates or anything else peculiar." Only Bert could use phrases like "case the joint" and not sound ridiculous.

We had several survivors in Israel, Canada, and the United States who were prepared to testify about Osidach's role in the roundups of Rawa-Ruska's Jews, but the accounts were sketchy or were provided by witnesses who were now aging or frail. We needed Sarowycz to support those accounts. But he was wily. After the war, he and his wife had made it into a DP camp in Germany, and on his application for a US visa, he had said he'd been a clerk during the war years.

According to the 1948 Displaced Persons Act, applicants could not enter the country if they had rendered "assistance to the enemy in the persecution of civilians." Any assistance to the SS, whose insignia was the skull and bones of their intended victims, reeked of "assistance to the enemy in the persecution of civilians." But the courts seemed likely to be reluctant to construe the law too broadly. Between the spectrum of those who pulled the trigger and those accused of having been much less than actual killers — translators and other low-level assistants — the courts would have to set limits, but it seemed a long-shot that it would encompass Sarowycz's activities. We could also charge him for not disclosing his true activities on his visa application, but we would also have to assert that had those activities been revealed, they would have prompted questions, which might or might not have sufficed to bar his entry into the United States.

All of this meant we had scant legal leverage against Sarowycz.

Bert parked the car behind Sarowycz's house and placed his hands on the steering wheel. "Mind if I have another smoke?" he asked. He was stalling, and I didn't mind.

"It's never easy to turn someone," he said warily. "Your first run at this. Mine too, with this crowd. But I've seen my share of bad guys."

"He's got to be led to believe," I said, "that we'll charge him, like Osidach, if he doesn't play ball. He'll say he was no chief of police. A translator. At worst, a transmitter of SS orders. So, he'll be betting that's not enough for willful assistance in persecution."

"But Allan," Bert interjected. "A translator and a transmitter? I may not have gone to Yale Law, but that sounds to me like 'assistance,' as you lawyers put it."

"We'll see. We're going into uncharted waters. Point is, we have to make him believe he *can* be deported if he doesn't cooperate."

Bert stamped out his cigarette. "Okay, let's do it," he said.

We quietly closed the car doors behind us.

An elderly woman dressed head-to-toe in black opened the door on the first ring. Her salt-and-pepper hair was pulled back in a low, neat bun. A single string of freshwater pearls shimmered against her dark tunic, giving her a look of harsh elegance and royal annoyance at the impertinence of our call.

"I am Mrs. Sarowycz," she said. "We have been expecting you." She pointed her freshly manicured fingers, nails painted blood red, toward the dining room table. A crystal pitcher filled with water and three matching glasses sat waiting for us: a picture of normalcy.

She motioned me to one of the dining room chairs facing a window looking out on the immaculate garden. At the garden's center was a precisely pruned pomegranate tree, about six feet tall, its fruit ready for harvest, smooth-skinned, brownish-red spheres bursting like ornaments from its verdant branches. Mr. and Mrs. Sarowycz apparently had no children, and I can't recall seeing any photographs, except an old framed picture that seemed to be of one of their parents. Their home seemed devoid of emotion, as if it all had been spent on their garden.

I sat down as directed. Bert moved quickly to the seat across from mine. We had gone over the tactics of the meeting several times to ensure that Sarowycz would be forced to sit between us.

As Bert explained, "You put the target of the investigation between yourself and your partner so that he can't keep an eye on both of you. That leaves the interrogators free to signal to each other without detection."

Mrs. Sarowycz excused herself. "My husband will be right down, gentlemen," she said flatly. "He is putting some documents together."

Bert and I opened our briefcases and took out our paperwork as well as the photo spread from which he had already made the identification. Maents later, he appeared, coming down the stairs spryly, aged gracefully.

"Good morning, gentlemen," he said, rolling the word "morning" as he walked slowly into the dining room. He looked remarkably similar to his image in the photo spread. His face was lined, his hair streaked with gray and white. But this was certainly the same man.

With a distinct Slavic accent, spoken with the refined charm of the paper-goods salesman he had once been, he began with an apology.

"Sorry for having kept you waiting. What is it that I can do for you?" As he spoke, he laid on the table a bundle of index cards carefully secured with a rubber band. It reminded me of the way my father bundled information.

Bert began: "Mr. Sarowycz, you remember me, from our last encounter when you were shown the photo spread."

"Of course I remember. You are the investigator."

"Yes. But this time I wanted you to meet Mr. Gerson, the attorney with responsibility for this case. As you know, it concerns the Osidach matter."

Bert cast me a glance indicating it was my turn take over.

"Good morning, Mr. Sarowycz," I said. "The US Government, through the Justice Department's Office of Special Investigations, is interested in obtaining further information about Mr. Wolodymir Osidach, whom I believe you know."

Sarowycz looked nervously about the room as if searching for his wife, but she had already gone upstairs or perhaps was leaning against the wall to catch what was being said.

"You should know," I said, staring at him directly, "that we believe we already have enough information to institute proceedings to strip Osidach of his US citizenship. But we want to make our case as strong as possible. So anything you can tell us about him will be appreciated." I took a deep breath. "I should also tell you that you yourself are under investigation for your activities during World War II."

"*What* activities?" Whether calculated or improvised, his emphasis on "W*hat*" resounded with defiance, if not contempt.

"I'll get to that in a moment," I said, "but first some preliminaries. If this were a normal criminal investigation, I would read you your rights."

Sarowycz adjusted the collar of his shirt.

"But this is not a normal criminal investigation," I said. "This is an immigration fraud matter, and you are by law required to answer the questions I pose to you. Any false answers will constitute a federal offense."

"A federal offense?"

"Yes, we are investigating whether you, in addition to Mr. Osidach, committed immigration fraud when applying for a U.S. visa, a fraud you repeated when you applied for US citizenship."

"I don't understand," he said.

"U.S. citizenship is granted only to people who have a lawful entry visa, issued on the basis of honest answers to prior questioning. Do you understand?"

"I understand very well," he said slowly. Then added: "You are threatening me?"

I held back from responding, realizing that he might be hoping for a rushed response that he could use later to argue that we had coerced his testimony.

He broke the silence, but now in a more defensive tone. "I have always told the truth. I love America. I didn't lie on my immigration or citizenship papers."

"We're not so sure about that," I said calmly.

Then, unexpectedly, he caved. "About Osidach, I am ready to cooperate."

"Fully?"

"Yes," he responded, "but there is not much I know. I am afraid that I cannot be of much help to you. If you have something specific to ask, ask me. I have nothing to hide."

He crossed his hands nervously, and then uncrossed them and

laid them on the table, palms facing upward. "Let's please get this unpleasantness over with."

He must have realized that he had more to gain by cooperating than stonewalling. For my part, I realized that it was time to soften my approach.

"Please bear in mind that we are principally interested in Mr. Osidach, not in you," I said. "But if you cooperate, that will be appreciated. If you choose not to cooperate, there will be consequences." I let the meaning of the words settle in. "Do you understand?"

"Perfectly," he said.

"Are you ready to talk?"

"As I said, I have nothing to hide."

I steadied myself and then moved to the heart of the matter. "What do you know of Osidach?"

"I know he was Rawa-Ruska's chief of police. I know he had about 15 auxiliary policemen under him."

"Did you work with him?"

"No."

"Never?"

"Never."

"Bert, hand me document number 21." I pointed across the table. "That folder there." He slid the papers toward me. I opened the folder to the first page, embossed with the seal, "Lviv Archives of the Great Patriotic War, Union of Soviet Socialist Republics."

"Do you see your name on this document?"

He took the paper and looked it over, betraying no emotion. "Yes, that looks like my name at the bottom. I also notice that it has the Soviet stamp from the Lviv Archives."

"What does the document say to you?"

"It lists the payroll."

"Whom is it signed by?"

"By SS Gauleiter Gerhart Strumpf."

"And who was he?"

"The SS chief in the Rawa-Ruska region." He laid the document back on the table, pushing it away from him. "What does that have to do with me?"

"Do you remember him?"

"Of course."

"People say that you acted as the liaison between him and Osidach. Is that true?"

"That is a lie," he snarled.

"Mr. Sarowycz, I must remind you that …"

With a quick movement of his right hand, he searched inside his jacket pocket. He pulled out a small plastic pillbox.

"You should know that giving false statements to a federal official, whether made under oath or not, is a crime, a federal offense."

He opened the pillbox and extracted a single tablet. I stopped speaking as he swallowed the pill with some water.

"Is that clear? Regardless of whether you committed immigration fraud, lying to a government official about a related matter, even though implicating someone else, is a crime."

He nodded, placing his hand on his chest. "Excuse me. It's nitroglycerin. I take it for my heart." He said it with an awkward half-smile. "Whether I need it, only God knows. One doctor says yes, another says no."

"We're sorry if this is distressing to you. My father takes nitroglycerin pills too. But we need to get the facts straight. Are you ready to go on?"

"Okay, yes." he said meekly.

"Let's start again. What was your connection to Osidach?"

"I was a translator. Sometimes they used me as a messenger too."

"They?"

"The Germans," he sighed. "I had studied German and French along with Philosophy in Rawa-Ruska. When I graduated, my uncle, who was the municipal clerk, hired me as a translator. I worked for him until I moved to Lviv. In 1939, I came back and worked for the municipality of Rawa-Ruska again until 1942."

He stopped, bringing his hands to his forehead and moving his fingers to his temples, and he seemed to swallow heavily before he continued. "By then, the Germans had taken control of the city." He placed his elbows on the table. "And of course, you know there was *no way* to refuse when they wanted you to serve at their headquarters. It was in the same building, the top two floors."

"By 'the Germans,' I take it you mean the SS and the Gestapo," I said.

"Yes. That is correct."

I scooped a handful of documents from the manila folder and pushed another sheet of paper across the table. "You submitted this in 1948 to the US consular office in Munich. Do you recognize it?"

"Yes. It is my visa application."

"Read, if you would, what you said in response to Item Number 4, which requires applicants to list all activity engaged in between 1939 and 1945. Also, please read your response to Item Number 6, which asked whether the applicant ever engaged in or assisted in the persecution of civilians on account of race, religion, creed, or national origin."

"I wrote 'secretary' to Question Number 4," he said, pointing to one of the documents. "That's true. I was a secretary. And I wrote 'no' to Question Number 6. That is also true."

"But the Gestapo and the SS had their offices in the old municipal building, and you worked for them. What did you do?"

"Secretarial work. And some translating."

"So, you think being a secretary and a translator are the same?"

"Well, no. Of course not." He shut his eyes and then rubbed them, as if exhausted by the exchange.

"And what did you translate for them?"

"German proclamations mostly, into Polish. Sometimes Polish documents or letters into German."

"Wasn't translation, in fact, your full-time job?"

"There was enough translation to keep me busy."

My efforts weren't bearing fruit. I needed to sharpen my questioning. "What did you do before the war? How did you get connected to the SS and Gestapo in the first place?"

"I was a law student in my second year at the University of Lviv, and when the war broke out, I headed back to Rawa-Ruska."

"How old were you at the time?"

"Twenty-five."

"And you were good with languages?"

"Yes. I already told you that," he answered impatiently.

"And you also said you were more than a secretary."

"Yes. I was a translator. But I was a secretary, too. I was... how do you say... 'predominantly' a translator."

He lingered on the word "predominantly," as if to convey that his language skills had been exaggerated.

"Did you translate documents that dealt with the liquidation of the Jews of Rawa-Ruska?"

"I don't remember."

I knew that German orders were unlikely to announce annihilation plans but would be couched as mere relocation edicts. The meaning, however, would be apparent to anyone working with the German SS.

"Do you know how many Jews lived in Rawa-Ruska before the war?"

"Fifteen thousand maybe."

"Fifteen thousand, and you don't remember whether you translated documents calling for their extermination?"

"It wasn't like that, Mr. *Gerzon*." He slowly pronounced my family name with a "z" instead of an "s," as if intended to show that he knew I had a personal history in the region. Gerzon was a popular Polish-Jewish name.

"The Germans never issued a proclamation calling for extermination. Not any that were shared with me," he said.

"Okay, then what other documents did you see or translate about the roundups?"

"Let me say it again: I never knew of the death camps until after the war." He took up the copy of his visa application and held it in both hands. "Orders I translated would merely call for Jews to assemble in the central square," he said. "They were issued in Osidach's name in Polish because he was chief of police, and also in German under the stamp of the SS Gauleiterde. From there the Jews would be taken to the station so they could be put on trains headed for the labor camps." He held out his hands as he spoke as if to proclaim his helplessness. "That's all I knew. Not very pleasant, but Polish gentiles were being sent away too. I did not know of extermination camps. And, as far as I know, neither did Osidach."

Not very pleasant, his words resonated in my ears.

"Labor camps? What did you take that to mean?" I asked, trying to stay calm.

"Just what I said. We believed they were being sent to work. You have to remember that Poles and Ukrainians also got sent to factories and mines in Germany. So yes, I translated documents instructing Jews to gather at the central square in Rawa-Ruska. So what?"

"So what?" I repeated slowly. "They were being sent to the gas chambers."

"Maybe so. But I had nothing to do with that. Why are you people making so much of this, so many years later? Why am I, a quiet old man, suddenly of such interest to the US Justice Department?"

Sadly, I realized that his befuddlement as to why the government would have any interest in his past was not feigned. He honestly seemed at a loss to understand what was wrong in enabling the extermination of Jews when the prize for this unseemly task was furthering the prospects for Ukrainian independence.

I continued: "As I said, our concern is misrepresentation. You said nothing on your visa application about translating roundup orders for the SS and Gestapo, ordering all Jews to the *Umschlagplatz*. Correct?"

"Yes, because I didn't think it mattered. It was a form of secretarial work, and I said I was a secretary."

"And you also swore you never assisted in persecution, and you must know that your work with the SS was a form of assistance."

"It was not."

"Well, like I said, my primary interest, and that of OSI, is in Mr. Osidach. Have you talked to him in recent years?"

"It was only a translation job."

"You're avoiding the question. Have you talked to him?"

"No! I haven't. I hear he is living in Philadelphia, but I never see him."

"Never?"

He let out a quiet groan, shrugging his shoulder. "Well, maybe once at a gathering of the OUN, the Organization of Ukrainian Nationalists."

"When?"

"In New York, about twenty years ago."

"Let's get back to the war years. Did you ever see Mr. Osidach at these roundups or anywhere ordering the men under his command to gather Jews for deportation?"

"No. I only saw his posted orders. I did not see him actually instructing people to do such things. But he was chief of police, you see, so everyone would see him around the city."

"And you say you attended an OUN rally in the 1950s because you, like Mr. Osidach, were a member of the OUN in the Ukraine."

"Yes, even before the war began. We wanted independence for the Ukraine. Surely you don't think there's anything wrong with that."

"No, I suppose not, unless you were willing to trade cooperation with the Nazis for the sake of ending Soviet control of Ukraine. Tell me, what were the aims of OUN?"

"The name spells it out, Mr. *Gerzon*," he said, again emphasizing the "z" sound. "The Organization of Ukrainian Nationalists is our national organization for the liberation of Ukraine."

"Liberation from whom?"

"From the Soviet Union, of course."

"And the Germans promised you independence for Ukraine — self-determination, national liberation – once they conquered Russia."

"Would you have chosen to live under Joseph Stalin's rule?"

That was a telling comment, as it spoke to his motivation for his assisting the Nazis. I knew he would never acknowledge that explicitly, but I continued, my tone even: "Independence for Ukraine was conditioned, of course, on the Ukrainians helping the Nazis, and that's why you helped them. Isn't that true?"

"It's not like you make it sound."

"And wasn't the OUN sympathetic to the Nazis' plan to rid Ukraine of its Jewish population?"

"You're twisting things around. We all knew that the Jewish intellectuals in Ukraine before the war were Bolsheviks and Communists. The OUN was against them because they were Communists, not because they were Jews."

"And you assisted, did you not, in the roundup of Jews for deportation to extermination camps?" Even as I asked the question, I knew that Sarowycz was not about to incriminate himself, not after having fielded everything else I had thrown his way.

"I don't know what you mean when you say I cooperated. I was a translator, a secretary. I did not even know of any extermination camps."

"Were you not present at the roundups of Jews?"

"No. Never. That was a local police function."

"People say they saw you with Osidach at the time."

"Who says that? It is not true!"

"But you admit to having translated and transmitted orders for the roundups even though, as you put it, you might not have known of the intended final destination."

"You make it sound like I was a military man giving orders. I translated, that's all. That was my job. I don't know what you mean when you say 'transmitted.' When I finished my translations, I gave them to the Germans or to the police chief, and I went home."

We were going around in circles. He must have realized that our ability to strip him of his US citizenship solely on the basis of translating Nazi orders—never directly couched as liquidation—was tenuous at best.

Of course, the bankers who funded the Nazis—the ones Rockler had tried at Nuremberg—hadn't fired a shot either. So, it remained plausible that based on the facts as he admitted, he too would face denaturalization.

"I understand that you and your wife may be moving to Florida soon. Is that true?"

Surprised by my sudden shift in tone, he seemed to relent. "Yes, we are going to Venice, on the west coast. I hear the fishing is good there," he said with a forced smile.

"I've heard that too."

"And it is very pleasant there." He gestured toward the pomegranate tree in the garden, indicating that he spent a good deal of time there. "Beautiful gardens and flowers."

"I can see why you would think about the flowers and gardens in Venice. You appreciate such things."

"In Rawa-Ruska, we had beautiful gardens," he said. "Everybody liked to garden, especially me. I always have, since I was a small boy. In the market in Rawa-Ruska, people would come up from Georgia with exotic plants and fruits, and the most exotic, I always thought, were the pomegranate trees with their big ripe fruit and hundreds of seeds." He nodded toward me. "Are you familiar with them?"

"I know them, yes."

"So, when we bought this house here, I planted a pomegranate tree right away, in the center of the garden. It's 15 years old."

"Then you should find Florida agreeable. But you should be prepared for a follow-up visit. You see, translating orders for the roundup of Jews being sent to extermination camps—or even labor camps, as you like to put it—remains inconsistent with what you said on your US visa application."

"I didn't lie."

"We'll let an immigration judge decide what kind of secretary you really were. But I don't think any US consular official would have admitted you if you had told them that during the war you were a secretary to the SS and Gestapo."

"All I was doing was working for them. I had to."

"Yes, and that fact, had you revealed it, would have disqualified you from entry into America."

"This isn't fair."

"So, I ask you again, is there anything else you wish to tell us at this time about what you observed Mr. Osidach doing? Do you know anything else about his responsibilities as chief of police in rounding up Rawa-Ruska's Jews? Can we call on you for testimony?"

"I have told you everything I know."

I gave Bert a nod to begin gathering our documents. The session was over, but I had one last question. "Tell me, Mr. Sarowycz, did you enjoy your job as a translator?"

He was taken aback. "Enjoy? We did what we had to do to survive, to maintain ourselves as the vanguard to one day throw off the oppressive Russians from the Ukrainian people. Now, Mr. *Gerzon*, may I ask you something?"

"Of course."

"You don't really know much about Ukrainian history, do you?"

"I know enough. Why do you ask?"

"Because if you knew Ukrainian history, you would know that we too were victims, like the Jews. You are Jewish, aren't you?

"Yes, I am," I said, caught off-guard.

"And I suppose you weren't born here."

What was he getting at?

"Mr. Sarowycz, I am a trial attorney, a law enforcement official with the US Department of Justice. Where I was born is hardly your concern."

"It might explain to me why you're asking me these questions."

"What is of concern is that you were not born here, you chose to immigrate here, and you withheld crucial information. You misrepresented certain facts on your immigration application. That's all."

"I only mean to point out that Osidach, like you, was a law enforcement official. He did his duty, and he had no choice. If he didn't follow the Germans' orders, he would have been shot. So would I, if I hadn't agreed to translate. And in the end, the Germans betrayed us."

Sarowycz shook his head, observing me coolly, as if I needed to be educated on the political facts of life. "And when America was forcibly repatriating us to the Soviet Union after the war, it knew we would be shot. So, what were we supposed to do? Let America betray us again? And after the war when Europe's Jews—maybe your own relatives—were guided to Israel or America, we Ukrainians were shipped by the hundreds of thousands back to Russia. Repatriated! Many committed suicide. They knew they would be shot or sent to prison, Russian prison, if sent back. Only because the Ukrainians were strong here in America, and united, was that... repatriation finally stopped."

He paused, and I decided to let him vent. I wanted to know his mindset. "We know what you are trying to do with Fedorenko and from where you get your information! From the Lviv Documentation Center. From the Soviet Union, America's enemy. From the Soviets! And you know the Soviets want that there should never be Ukrainian independence. That's why they are doing it. And isn't independence a cherished American value?"

"Not at any price," I said.

"I did not assist. Assist is what you do voluntarily. The war was thrust upon us."

"It's time to end this session, Mr. Sarowycz, Thank you for your time. I am sure we will be in touch. "

We showed ourselves out the door, past his beautiful pomegranate garden into the warm but welcome air of southern California.

Outside, Bert shook his head.

"Glad I'm not a lawyer," he said. "For me it's clear. Put the bastard away."

That wasn't the objective, of course, but I understood his frustration. On the one hand, we had not flipped Sarowycz—he did not say that he had seen Osidach round up and deport anyone. Even if we put him on the stand to testify that Osidach was indeed the police chief, we couldn't be certain that he would stick to that statement. But we had rattled him, and it was possible that he could still be useful down the road.

More important, at least for me, our meeting with Sarowycz was clarifying, as I felt I had learned something: what motivated people like Sarowycz to act as they did. He was not inherently anti-Semitic, no more than other Ukrainians disposed to co-exist with Jews. Rather, it was a matter of arithmetic. He believed the Jews were doomed anyway and that in 1941 and 1942, Nazi victory and domination of all of Europe was a near certainty; thus, his assistance with the Final Solution would make no difference, but it would provide the advantage of speeding independence for his country. That was his moral calculus. It was a calculus of evil, but not nearly as banal as Hannah Arendt's evil. Sarowycz's calculus was self-exonerating, nationalistic, and diabolical.

Our meeting was a piece of the larger puzzle that I craved to understand. I knew that my colleagues had a different perspective on that history, but I still felt that we were all on the same track.

And if Bert had pulled out his revolver and taken a shot at the pomegranate tree, I would have been okay with that as well.

Sam, Paula, Morton and Allan Gerson, December 1950, on the train to Bremen.

Chapter Ten

Never Forget, Never Forgive

Upon entering America, we had to clear the US Customs Service. I have no memory of that experience, but it did produce a document itemizing my parents' belongings. They included a table, four chairs, bedding, towels, cutlery, and some other items whose value totaled $45.75. (The list did not include Ma's sewing machine, which she also brought with her.) According to a social welfare agency record at the time they had "almost $30" when they arrived in America.

We initially received help from the Hebrew Immigrant Aid Society (HIAS), which had offices across Europe (including Foehrenwald), and played a huge role in helping refugees reach America, and provided further assistance in helping them assimilate. A member from HIAS drove us to the Astor Mansion on 425 Lafayette Street in Lower Manhattan. Originally converted to a spacious public library that served as an intellectual center of the city, the building was acquired by HIAS and used to shelter new immigrants. Its high ceilings and palatial aura made it seem as if we were indeed in some other world. No one in our family spoke English, so we obtained some English primer books, and my mother and I would study together. One day we came across a strange word that defied phonetic translation. My mom kept pronouncing it as *lag-heh*. An older woman who worked in the building had taken us under her wing, and when she stopped by, we asked her about the word. It was "laugh," and when she told us the pronunciation, all we could do was, well, laugh.

The Astor Mansion was temporary housing, and I had forgotten that I had once lived there until more than two decades later, in 1968. I was a law student, and I attended a play by the New York

Shakespeare Festival. I felt terribly distracted throughout. My date asked me why, and I finally understood after I walked into the lobby and saw a plaque on the wall commemorating this very building as the site that HIAS used to shelter immigrants after the Second World War.

From a beloved athenaeum to a sumptuous refugee shelter to *King Lear*: America, always reinventing itself.

In our first days in New York, we went to see my cousin Sol and his parents, who had arrived in America a year before we did. They lived in a tenement, which faced another tenement. The rooms were crowded and dark, and I couldn't help but think about the fresh air, open space, and verdant environs of Foehrenwald. "This is America?" I asked. Sol taunted me in Yiddish, "*Greeneh, Greeneh,*" or greenhorn, and I looked at my skin.

My parents faced two urgent tasks—finding a place to live and finding employment, and in both efforts, they received assistance from the Jewish Social Services Association, which provided aid to new families. The social workers had several meetings with my parents and produced detailed, typewritten reports, in which my dad was described as "an adequate self-directing person who seems to be extremely intelligent," and my mom was "very presentable" and a "gray-haired charming looking woman with a warm, direct manner."

The travel and travails of the past decade had taken a physical toll on my father, who, now 45-years-old, had serious back pain; at Foehrenwald, it was diagnosed as a "ruptured intervertebral disc" and in New York as a "lumbar-spine condition." Whatever it was, it complicated my dad's already difficult job prospects, the language barrier being just one of the challenges. My dad took great pride in his bookkeeping acumen, but those accounting skills applied to businesses in Poland and other European countries. They were useless in America. Despite his brief foray as a Siberian lumberjack, he was also not equipped for heavy physical labor. The Jewish social services agency found him a factory job, which paid thirty cents an hour. But it required him to stand, and when he asked to sit, the foreman told him no. He lasted one day.

Meanwhile, my mother's sewing machine had a broken motor, and she could not afford to replace it, so she too was stymied.

Apartment hunting was equally difficult. The agency gave my

parents several leads on apartments. In one case, my dad arrived after it had already been taken. In another instance, he reached the apartment but didn't want to take it until my mom had seen it. By the time she arrived, it was taken. They had an opportunity for yet another apartment, but it cost $60 a month. Even with financial assistance from the agency, that was too expensive. My mom also made clear that she would not consider any unheated apartments: she feared, always, that her children's lives were at risk.

Two months after we arrived at the Astor mansion, in February 1951, my parents found an apartment on 84 Beaver Street in the Bushwick section of Brooklyn. It was on the fourth floor, which was a drawback, but it had four rooms, was airy, and, at $39 a month, affordable. The neighborhood wasn't the best, but it served our purposes. An open poultry market was down the street, and my mother would buy the chickens, pluck them, put them in the bath, clean them, and cook them.

My father had a wealthy cousin, Morris, who lived in West Hempstead, on Long Island, and in time we would visit him in his mansion (or at least that's what it felt like to us). A relative could sponsor an immigrant's entry into the United States, but Morris was the one who had a criminal record for tax evasion, so he could not serve that role for my dad. He could, however, give my dad a job at his factory in the garment district, cutting drapes and bedspreads and lifting heavy bales of linen. It was a mixed blessing. The job generated income but made my dad's bad back even worse and frustrated him personally. His mind was his greatest asset, but he could no longer use it to make a living. His back eventually gave out while lifting a bolt of yarn, and after surgery and several hospitalizations, he could no longer work in Morris's factory. In 1961, while also collecting workers' compensation, my dad got a job as a sales clerk in a candy and luncheonette store for $45 a week. It kept him busy, but hardly satisfied.

Both my parents took English classes at night, though my mom more fully embraced assimilation. She also got her sewing machine fixed and was soon doing piecemeal work in our walkup tenement for a fabric sweatshop in the neighborhood. I watched her sew with care and precision, accompanied by the sing-song humming of the needle, and I recognized how closely machine and person were intertwined, the source of income and security, threading our family's path through its next crucible.

My parents sent me to a yeshiva, even though they themselves were not observant. The death camps had made them overtly suspicious of God's benevolent attention to his "chosen people." For my mother in particular, the sense of abandonment could never be assuaged. *How could God have let so many perish?* My mom hated even the mention of God in our home. Nonetheless, my parents sent me to a yeshiva, in part to keep me off the streets, but also to fulfill my father's desire that I understand my Jewish roots. Our literature, our poetry, and our language—as well as our history—were all beautiful and all worth knowing and preserving.

I spent many hours mastering my secular as well as religious studies, but I lived in disconnected worlds. My teacher was a tall rabbi in a black frock suit. Once, he slammed his long wooden ruler across my knuckles when he caught me staring at a comic book that I had placed between the pages of the prayer book that I was supposed to be studying. During the day, I learned about being a good kosher boy, and then in the evening, I watched my mom pour milk into the mashed potatoes and serve them with meat. When I asked her about this, she said, "Yes, *Ellenu*, but it was just a little milk."

I acquired an immigrant boy's diligence in acclimation and sense of purpose. My hero was the Dodger's Duke Snyder, and my overriding ambition was to blend in as quickly as possible, to lose my accent, to catch a hard drive in right field, and, as a teenager, to learn the Lindy, perchance to have a girlfriend. On my daily mission to the candy store, I bought my dad's Yiddish newspapers, *The Forward* and *Der Tag*, but I hid them in my copy of *The Brooklyn Eagle* so the other boys wouldn't see them.

After three years in Brooklyn, and with my parents concerned about tensions in the neighborhood, we moved to the Bedford Park section of the Bronx, and there our finances eventually improved when my parents opened a dry-cleaning and tailoring store. They turned that into a dressmaking shop as well, run by my mother, whose spirits were buoyed when she walked down Fifth or Madison Avenues to evaluate the storefronts showcasing the latest fashions that she could incorporate into her work. The store would provide my parents with modest but steady income until their retirement.

The perception of the Bronx, then and now, is that it's a depressed community. But it wasn't for us, and it was certainly an upgrade from Brooklyn, as we now lived just a few blocks away from the New York Bronx Botanical Gardens.

As if by magic, we now had one of the world's finest public gardens in our backyard. Every Sunday, weather permitting, we made our pilgrimage there—230 acres of rolling country, including the Bronx River with a dramatic 75-foot gorge, a virgin hemlock forest, a lush Rose Garden, and an Italian Renaissance Museum, with a 308-foot front façade. It was a slice of the Old Country—a reminder for my father, I'm certain, of the spas outside of Zamość.

We would often go with one of my mom's friends from Romania, Eva Nadelstern and her husband Mark, who were also Holocaust survivors, and we'd sit on a bench beyond the large greenhouses. There, my mother held court on the apparel of anyone in our midst, but particularly the women of style: did they have the appropriate dress length (fourteen inches from the hem, if memory serves); did they have raglan sleeves or ones without cushions; was their palette of colors elegantly coordinated; was the fabric ordinary or inspired; were the accessories bold or timid? We would go inside the greenhouses for a while, and the humidity felt good on cold days.

But we mainly sat outside on the bench and watched the parade, and my mom's running commentary was similar to her observations at museums. She focused on the frill collars in Renaissance paintings and wondered aloud how one could use white paint on a white canvas. But she was more than just an observer: She was an artist herself. At home she used charcoals to draw pictures of Spanish-style colonial homes with protruding wooden beams, and of Spanish women in traditional dress. She liked charcoal, I believe, because it was similar to the chalk she used in dressmaking, and she later drew in colored pencils. I also believe that she favored the Spanish-style homes because they reminded her of the Renaissance-style squat buildings of Zamość, while she drew the Spanish women because of their elegance.

It was clear to me, even as a kid, that my mom's passion for art and design was more than just her vocation or hobby. It was also a way for her to cope with all that she had lost, an outlet, an escape into a universe that she could control and perfect. It allowed her to convey to her children the beauty of the world, however frayed its edges, however cruel its betrayals.

My father was much stricter than my mother, much less communicative, more prone to outbursts. He internalized his despair, until it erupted. His damaged back factored into these moods. The stress points multiplied, and I rarely knew what he was thinking.

I once asked him, "Why are you so angry?"

He responded in Yiddish: "If you need to ask, it's no good already."

"I'm not a prophet," I said. "How can I know what you're thinking?"

"You got to just know."

My father coped by maintaining his connections to his past, in part by reading Yiddish newspapers and books and by reaching out to Yiddish poets in New York. More important, he became part of the Zamość Memorial Society. Most towns in Poland, and many throughout Europe, had Memorial Societies, led by the scattered Jewish remnant seeking to preserve shards of memory and to honor the dead. Their sacred task was usually to create memorial books.

That was true of the diaspora from Zamość, whose members by the 1950s stretched to the United States, Canada, Israel, Argentina, Bolivia, and Australia. A number of Jews from Zamość had immigrated to Buenos Aires before the war, including two of my mother's brothers, and the memorial book was the brainchild of the Argentine cohort. Subcommittees were created; all members from all countries were asked to contribute letters, photographs, and remembrances, and the book took seven years to assemble and distribute.

It was a triumph of graphic production and photocopying as well as artistic vision. The cover is black, and inscribed on the bottom, in bright orange Yiddish letters, is "Zamość," and rising from the letters are dramatic orange flames, on which is written the Yiddish word for "Annals."

The *Annals of Zamość* contains 1,200 pages of names, memories, photographs, stories, and prayers. Printed on the final page are these words:

Never, never will we forget our holy martyrs.
Never, never will we forgive their murderers.

Those words were quite familiar to me, as they were used in creating a Zamość memorial site at a cemetery in New Jersey. Its goal was to honor the Jews of Zamość who were killed in the Holocaust. The project began in 1953, and my father worked on it seemingly every night. I used to translate Yiddish into English for my dad, and one day he asked me to translate a phrase that would be inscribed on the giant headstone.

The phrase was: *Never forget. Never forgive.*

"Never?" I asked him. "Isn't that too strong?"

My dad all but spat out the answer. "No! It's not too strong!"

The memorial was unveiled in 1958. Trucks hauled in two loudspeakers for the presentation, and my cousin Sol and I were among those who addressed the crowd. Whatever I said is long forgotten, but not so my dad's contribution: His name is engraved on the headstone as the secretary of the memorial committee.

Honoring the past bordered on obsession for my parents. We'd go to large auditoriums in the Murray Hill area of Manhattan and attend remembrances of the Warsaw Ghetto Uprising in 1943: a stirring tribute to heroism and defiance. The Jewish insurgents refused to surrender to deportation, took up arms against the SS, inflicted significant casualties, and fought valiantly for nearly a month before succumbing. At these gatherings in Manhattan, Jewish immigrants stood up to celebrate the valor of the ghetto warriors: how they fought back and held off the Wehrmacht, with some resisters escaping through the sewers, and what must it have felt like to emerge from that manhole!

What I most remember were the people standing and singing loudly "The Partisan Fighter's Song," which was written by a Jewish inmate in the Vilna Ghetto after he heard about Warsaw. The opening line says: "Never say you are going down the last road, for our sought-after hour will yet come." The song became an anthem for my parents and for Holocaust survivors everywhere, sung at memorial services all over the world. In my mind, the song merged with the martial music of "Victory at Sea," the documentary that I so avidly watched of World War II battles.

Allan, his wife Joan and daughter Daniela, circa 1979.

Chapter Eleven

Leap of Faith

Sarowycz wasn't our only lead in identifying Osidach. We believed we had help in Israel.

As part of his investigation, Bert Falbaum had spoken with Israeli police about several Holocaust survivors who had been in Rawa-Ruska during the war but now lived in Tel Aviv. The police had spoken with them and shared their notes with Bert, who gave them to me. It was a promising enough lead for me to fly there myself in October 1979.

I met my counterparts in the Israel Police Department's permanent unit dedicated to finding Nazi criminals, some of whom they sent to Germany for trial. These officials worked in a ramshackle building, with a sign in Hebrew that read *"Snif L'Poshim Nazim"*: "Branch for Nazi Criminals." But OSI's proceedings were a different matter, as we eschewed the word "criminal." In focusing on immigration fraud, our proceedings were significantly more civil than criminal, requiring a much lower standard of proof than that which routinely pertains in criminal trials. Moreover, we were not pursuing actual Nazis who had committed actual war crimes, but their enablers or collaborators. Nonetheless, the Israelis proved helpful in tracking down witnesses through the head of the office, Lieut. Col. Menachem Russek.

Over the next three days, I took taxis to three different homes of men who had been in Rawa-Ruska and who had glimpsed Osidach in his blue police uniform and blue hat. One of the men had a very clear image of him, which could be useful in a trial. But none of them saw Osidach organizing the roundup and dispatching Jews. That was disappointing, but I was perhaps even more disappointed when I was interviewing one of the survivors, who was telling me about what he saw and how he persevered, and two of his children were sitting in an adjacent room watching Wimbledon, the volume turned up. They had no interest in their father's story.

The following months, back in the United States, I sent my recommendations to Rockler, urging that we bring denaturalization proceedings against Osidach for orchestrating the deportation of Rawa-Ruska's 18,000 Jews and lying about that involvement on his visa. I noted that our success depended on the quality of the witness statements we could obtain to supplement our documentary evidence. In this regard, I wrote that Sarowycz was an unreliable witness, and that initial feeling was only buttressed by my depositions of him, with co-counsel Norman Moscowitz, in Sarasota, Florida, in May 1980.

We had one more card to play against Osidach, and I would need my dad to help me play it.

Given Rawa-Ruska's proximity to Zamość, I called my dad to see if he had any suggestions. Whatever misgivings he had about my working at OSI or about OSI's objectives, he still wanted me to succeed, and he drew on his own network to find a Rawa-Ruska chapter of Workmen's Circle, a Jewish cultural and fraternal organization founded at the turn of the century. The chapter was in New York, so I called its chairman, who invited me to meet with him in Manhattan.

The chapter was made up almost entirely of those who had left before the war or the handful who escaped just before the roundups began. I met the chairman at a restaurant on Thirty-Seventh Street, and he gave me a Rawa-Ruska memorial book—it was in the same spirit as the Zamość book, but far smaller; a touching gift nonetheless.

He told me about a woman named Ida Rybitwer, and she lived alone in Toronto, supported by some meager pension funds and minimal reparations she was receiving from the Federal Republic of Germany. She was a loner, he said. His organization had reached out to her, but she preferred her solitude. She might have seen Osidach, and she also had a survivor's story that few could match: she had jumped out of a train that was already in motion and heading to Belzec, splashing into the Bug River below.

I told him I'd give her a call.

On January 5, 1980, Bert and I, joined by Neal Sher, the new deputy director who would be in charge of the pre-trial preparations, flew into Toronto. We took a taxi to the city's Downsview section, where Ida (pronounced EE-da) had made her home since the early 1950s. She was a bit shaky in my conversation with her, but she also had valuable information. How well she could hold up to cross-examination was something we could only determine by seeing her in person. But Rockler had accepted my recommendation regarding Osidach, so now Ida's testimony would be critical.

Ida answered our knock on the second go-around. She looked older than I had imagined. Stooped and arthritic, clutching a cane, she was little more than five feet tall. Her face was dry as a weathered caked desert. Her eyeglasses were the over-sized, drugstore-variety type, worn slightly askew, tight on her nose, with the lenses visibly splotched with grime and fingerprints. Nothing about her evinced the young woman she had been, surviving by intuition and iron will.

The apartment was a study in monastic simplicity. The living room bookcase was filled with worn books and a row of Readers Digest condensed novels. The furniture consisted of an old gray sofa with a small round cocktail table. The lighting was dim, the curtains drawn, giving her place a perpetual haze.

She escorted us into the kitchen and pointed to three rickety wooden chairs. "Won't you sit down?" she asked, pointing to a table with chromed aluminum legs and a dark green linoleum tabletop. She turned on the adjustable reading lamp mounted on the wall above the table.

"I've got some coffee and raisin *rugelach*. Or would you prefer tea?"

"Coffee would be lovely, Ms. Rybitwer," Bert said.

Ida went to the stove, relying on the cane for balance. She poured water she had already boiled into a coffeepot with instant coffee. A plate of *rugelach*—small crescents made from butter, cream cheese, and flour and stuffed with walnuts, and raisins, straight out of my own family's ritual—followed.

We got down to business. Neal was prepared to let me take the lead and would only step in when clarification was required.

"I understand that you settled here in Toronto in the early 1950s," I began.

"Well, Mr. Gerson, after the war, my cousin Eliana invited me to join her in Toronto. It was fine for a while. I enjoyed being with her, and I found work as a librarian's helper. But the winters got colder, and my bones got older.

"So, you're retired now?"

I remember her bony fingers caressing the side of the saucer. "Well, I'm a *little tired,*" she responded after a moment's thought. "I am also *retired,*" she said, realizing the reason for our smile.

"Thank you. We appreciate your help, and we don't want to take up too much of your time. Would you mind if we begin by looking at some photographs?"

"I suppose that's alright." Ida sighed and then adjusted her glasses as if steadying herself for examining the photos to pick out the man we were pursuing. We had not given her notice that there would be a photo spread to examine. We wanted everything fresh, spontaneous, and certainly nothing on our part that might suggest whom we hoped she would identify.

"Please look through these pictures," I said, "and tell me if you recognize anyone. Take your time."

Ida took the photo spread into her hands, surveyed it for a moment, and laid it down.

"I realize they're from a long time ago," I said.

"I understand." She squinted through her thick eyeglasses as she peered at the images, studying each one as though it might carry some unwelcome secret. Suddenly she dropped the photo spread on the tabletop and took in a long, anxious breath. "That's him. That's Osidach! Osidach had the build of a powerlifter and the head of a bull."

"*Mamzer!*" Bastard, she exclaimed, as if her strength gathered with the flood of memory. Ida stared at the picture for a long moment, her fingers tapping rhythmically.

"Are you sure?" Bert interjected.

"*Believe me, I'm sure!*"

Neal perked up, and around this point our questions became interchangeable so I can only remember the gist of our questions, and of course her answers, but no longer precisely who was putting them forward.

"And the one you say is Wolodymir Osidach. What can you tell us about him?"

"He was the commandant. He would strut about in his cap and fancy blue police uniform with gold buttons."

"Did you ever see him at a roundup?"

"Yes. At the first big one. At the *Umshlagplatz*, the gathering point. That's where the trains were waiting, the trains for Belzec. He was there, commanding."

She took in a long breath. "That's where they herded up Rawa-Ruska's Jews, thousands of them." She turned the photospread toward me and pointed at Osidach. "His men marched us to the trains and shoved us in like sardines."

"And after that, did you see him again?"

"No." Ida placed her hands together and slowly lowered her head, closing her eyes for a moment.

"After that, I was in hiding." The fingers of her left hand gripped the fingers of her right. "And you know, before the war, I knew his wife." One hand caressed the back of the other, then moved to the palm. As her breathing quickened, I watched the way her jaws worked against each other and could not help but notice a veil of pain descend across her face. "She gave music lessons to my brother. A very nice lady."

This was promising. Ida could not only identify him but appeared to be a credible eyewitness to Osidach's role in leading the roundups.

"Do you mind a personal question?" I asked when there was a sudden lull in the conversation

Ida sat back, her white hair in soft contrast to the odd angle of her glasses. Summoning my best Yiddish, I asked: *"Wie host de genemt de koach, de globenicht, tze varfen sich von der bahn?"* "Where did you get the courage, the belief, the self-assuredness that led you to throw yourself out of that train? The train was going over the river, wasn't it, when you opened the window and jumped into the water?"

I sat back as if to soften the abruptness of the questions. "And you survived. What made you do it? No one else was jumping."

Ida had been surprised by my Yiddish. She reared her head and studied me, taking in every feature of my face as if trying to figure out my own background.

"You look like a gentile but you speak like a *Galicianer*," she responded, referencing the area straddling eastern Poland and Ukraine from which both our families originated.

"My parents are from Zamość, near Rawa-Ruska."

"Oh, Zamość. You don't have to tell me where Zamość is. It was very famous. Rosa Luxembourg, the Communist organizer was from there, and Yitzhak Peretz, you know, the, the..."

"The writer."

"You do know! Yes, he came from there, too. It was a town different than the others. Beautiful. It was an intellectual center."

"An artistic center as well, yes."

"That's right. So beautiful that..." Ida pursed her lips. "Heinrich Himmler himself... You know who I am talking about?"

"Of course, the head of the SS."

"That's right. Himmler himself fell in love with Zamość and wanted it renamed Himmlertown! They got rid of all the Jews, and then they kicked out all the gentile Poles to make way for ethnic Germans. Sent them to Auschwitz. I don't think they were sent to the gas chambers. But I think most of them must have perished there, too."

"I didn't know that about Zamość," I said. My father had never ever mentioned that to me.

"But I didn't answer your question, did I?" Ida asked. "What made me throw myself from the train?" She sighed. "The train was on the bridge over the river. I suddenly knew we were going to be killed. Don't ask me how. I just knew it in my heart. The men who rounded us up and pushed us to board the trains had assured us that we were headed to labor camps, not the extermination camp that was actually at the end of the thin new railroad tracks the Germans had built. We were crossing the Bug River toward Poland. It was a low bridge. We had all heard rumors of German '*vernichtungslager*,' extermination camps. If I had thought too much about it, I wouldn't have jumped. Why should the Germans want to kill all the Jews? It made no sense. But for whatever reason, maybe God knows, maybe He wasn't around that day, it became clear to me: The way they rounded us up, the way they packed us into the trains, it just became clear—very clear—that the Germans really meant to kill us: all of us, every one of us — children, mothers, no exceptions!"

"'Open the window,' I shouted. 'Open it!' We had been packed in so tight; it was unbearably crowded. You could hardly breathe. The others all said I was crazy." Ida stopped herself, as if, after all, why should they imagine the unimaginable? She lowered her voice.

"They all said I was crazy, but no one tried to stop me. No one.

Someone even helped me—a man I barely knew. We had only exchanged a few words before that. He'd been a textile merchant. I didn't really know anything else about him. But he helped me pry the window open."

She sighed again and continued. "He pushed me through, that fine man. My arm brushed against the bridge on the way down, and I thought I was done for as I fell into the river. It was terribly cold. I thought I would die right then, so cold." She gathered her arms before her and turned her head away from me, as though she were unable to tell me anymore. "You know, I fell maybe five feet to the edge of the bridge, then maybe fifteen feet to the river below. I was—how do you say it in English—battered? But I survived." She whispered: "I was a swimmer. I made it back to dry land."

But laying a hand on her abdomen, she said she had paid a price. "My insides were torn. I could never have children, a family of my own."

I suddenly felt that I had to move, to engage my hands and feet, my charged nerves. I began gathering up our papers.

"So, tell me," she said, "who was crazy? Eh? Tell me. Where are they all now?" she asked, her eyes fixed on the chipped tiles below our feet. "And here I am, talking to you, telling the story of Rawa-Ruska's Jews so many decades later."

"After you jumped from the train, you returned to Rawa-Ruska?" I asked.

"Yes, but not just yet." Ida excused herself mid-sentence, suddenly standing and walking into the living room without her cane. Ida returned, carrying a purse from which she pulled out her wallet and extracted a small, creased, sepia-toned photograph with serrated edges of a young man in an SS uniform. "This is Schmidt." She held it up in front of her, displaying it, her voice cracking as she spoke. "He saved us."

"An SS officer?" I took the photo from her. It showed Schmidt looking straight into the eye of the camera, the SS unit insignia of two small lightning strikes on his lapel, and that of the *totenkopf* on his officer's cap.

"I laid on the ground by the river until dark. I thought I would die of the cold, and my head was bleeding. My brother had told me that he would hide in a bunker, a kind of cave that he had carved out in the woods near our home. I was able to find it. And when I crawled inside, he wasn't there! But he had blankets, and had left stale cheese, and radishes."

"He left a note that said all the Jews had been deported. He had to leave to try to join up with some partisans and that if I made it to the hiding place that it wouldn't be long before the Germans discovered it." Ida took the photo back from me. "It is of an SS intelligence officer named Schmidt, who liked watches. And my brother said he was different from the rest. 'Schmidt might help you,' he said. "And he did, for a few days, but that's another story. Anyway, he disappeared. They sent him to the Eastern front. But I kept his picture. I don't want to talk about it anymore."

We paused, let her catch up with herself.

"Tell me about the rest of the war. How did you get out of Rawa-Ruska?"

"I passed for a good gentile girl." Ida reached up to adjust her hair. "I was a blonde. No one took me for a Jew. A Polish woman hid me, and then I found work here and there until I was shipped into Germany to work at a munitions factory. Another story."

Our talk was beginning to take a toll on her. Neal interjected saying we are preparing for a trial in Philadelphia in a few months time. I would like you to be available as a witness, to say no more than you told us now, although you will be subject to cross-examination to questioning by Osidach's lawyer. Do you think that is something you can do? We would of course take care of all expenses and arrangements."

"It's my duty, isn't it?" she said wanly.

We thanked her and stood up to leave. She put one hand on the kitchen table and the other on her cane, and then pushed her eyeglasses up the ridge of her nose, reverting to being a stooped, fragile old lady but not yet ready to be consigned to the ash bin of history, for she still had tell her story to tell, and to tell it where it mattered most, in a US courtroom.

We called for the taxi to take us back to our hotel. We had found the witness we needed. The question was whether she could summon the same strength when she took the stand.

77-6725 (2A-6B) 675M-3-54   142

LUBAVITCHER
P. S. YESHIVA   Borough Bronx

Board of Education
City of New York

Report Card

Term beginning Sept. 1955

Name Blumstein, Abraham

Class 6   Room

Teacher Mrs. Bottalico

TO PARENTS:

   The school is trying to aid the growth of your child in scholarship, in health habits and in character. To get the best results, inside and outside school, your help is needed.

   The principal and the teacher will be pleased to talk matters over with you.

Report card for Allan Gerson's alias, Abraham Blumstein, at Lubavitcher Yeshiva in the Bronx, 1955.

Chapter Twelve

True Identity

I always knew there were elements of my parents' lives that were sequestered, parts of their history that were too difficult to discuss or even acknowledge. I imagined that these stories, these deeper truths, lay in some imaginary box marked "Better Not To Know," and I assumed that any effort to jostle that box, to reveal its contents, would spill out more pain and sorrow than I had any right to inflict.

My parents, in fact, did have a box – it was actually a large drawer – that offered a glimpse into their past. The drawer was part of our oversized mahogany cocktail table, and it held a stack of black-and-white photographs from Zamość. Many were photographs whose clarity revealed that they had been taken by a large-format camera, probably by a professional. They depicted handsome, well-dressed men and women, friends and relatives of my parents as well as of my parents themselves, images of the town's beautiful architecture and streetscape and countryside. There was also a picture of my older brother Eric as a baby, held in my mother's arms.

I was mesmerized by these pictures, not only by their richness, but by the story behind their retrieval and preservation by my Aunt Raya who was actually my father's cousin, although I always addressed her as "Aunt." Born Rajna Grubman, she had grown up in Zamość and, after the city was occupied, might have suffered the same fate as all the others who remained were it not for her personal charm, independent streak, and beauty. (She always reminded me of Lauren Bacall).

As a single young woman of 19, she found herself in a tough position. After her mother's death, her father remarried and had a new baby. That household did not have space for her. Her only option was to go work as a nanny for her aunt, something that she did not want to do. In early 1940 the Germans had taken over full control of Zamość from the Red Army that had withdrawn to Ukraine. Along with 7,000 to 8,000 other Jews, Aunt Raya saw an opportunity to flee to Russia, escape the Germans and avoid the stifling fate of being a nanny, all in one fell swoop.

On her way, the train stopped at a juncture where the trains heading for Siberia also stopped. This was where she spotted my family's photographs in the bin and making use of her beauty and charm, retrieved them with the audacious ruse of asking the Russian guard to bring her a glass of water. Her grandfather was a doctor and she stuffed inside his doctor's satchel the photos.

Aunt Raya did make it to Russia. She learned the language, drove a tractor on farms, and met her first husband, Wolfgang Taub, a fellow refugee who was much older than she was. She endured starvation and typhus. She told us that people "were falling dead like flies in front of you." Yet through it all, she never lost hold of my family photos.

After the war, she returned to Poland and Austria and Germany in search of her family, stopping at the DP camps, which listed the names of their occupants. She also scoured the lists of survivors provided by the International Committee of the Red Cross and by the major American Jewish welfare organization operating in postwar Europe, the Joint Distribution Committee. Through the latter, she was able to find my parents at Foehrenwald. Once there she opened up the precious bundle she had held onto for years and let the contents, their photographs, spill out. She told me how my parents cried when they saw her, stunned by this miracle, but she was on her way once again.

She and Wolfgang had started a lingerie factory in Germany and had dreams of moving it to Israel. Alas, neither the marriage nor the business survived. However, Raya did manage to emmigrate to the U.S. She moved to New York around the same time we did. She settled in Manhattan and finally found her soul-mate—the renowned Bulgarian drummer, David Eskin (Eshkenazi), who himself had spent three years in German labor camps.

Theirs is a wild story with a happy ending. Raya and David married and had two daughters, and they found stability and bliss in America. I relished my visits with my aunt in her large pre-war apartment overlooking Riverside Drive, with framed photographs lining her walls, mostly of family members who had perished in the war. And the photographs she rescued for my parents served as a window for me into this whirlwind of tragedy, bearing witness in their sepia-toned and serrated edged images to a past that my parents could only haltingly convey.

My Yiddish name is "Elle." That's what my parents always called me, though my mom used "Ellenu," adding the lyrical "nu" to denote affection.

My American name was Abraham Blumstein. My parents and my brother Sam were also named Blumstein.

I had no memory of what our surname was in Foehrenwald, and I had no reason to think there was anything unusual about Blumstein. But there were some oddities about that name. My father's cousin on Long Island, for whom he worked, had a different last name than my father – he was Morris Gerson. But I never gave it a second thought. I also collected stamps as a kid, and we would get letters from my dad's brother in Israel. My younger brother, Sam, noticed that the return address had the name "Gerson." Sam asked my dad why his brother had a different name. My dad blanched, but never answered the question. Neither Sam nor I pursued the matter.

When I was about 12 years old, we were at the large Klein's Department Store on Union Square. It was winter, and my mom had bought me a scarf—a *shalikel*, as she called it in Yiddish. As we left Klein's, we saw a hot dog vendor, sauerkraut spilling from his cart, On spotting my dad, he yelled, "Mottel Gerson!" My dad seemed to panic. He curtly told my brother and me to wait behind while he and my mom spoke to the vendor. Hushed words were exchanged, and then they returned to us, visibly shaken. These were strange occurrences, but they were part of what went into that imaginary box of "Better Not To Know."

I respected my parents' secrets, or suspected secrets. I also assumed that I was Abraham Blumstein. But it was not my real identity. It was manufactured. I have no real memory of being told the truth other than that something happened in April, 1958 after going on the subway with my parents and getting out on at 42nd Street and then going into a lawyer's office. I had never been in a law office, and I remember looking at the diplomas on the wall and remembering the lawyer's name: "Kies." Unknown to me, my parents went to court with the lawyer. I recall sitting by myself, and I saw blue papers that folded in three (they were subpoenas), and I had a sense that this is what you serve people, and I thought—what power.

Everything else is a total blur, except after we got home, I now had to tell people that I had a new name. I was now Allan Gerson. I recall going to get a haircut, and my barber said, "Abie, how are you doing?"

I said, "I'm no longer Abie."

"What do you mean you're no longer Abie?"

I doubt that I had a good answer for him or for anyone else, and certainly for not my classmates.

When we moved to the Bronx three years earlier from Brooklyn, I was enrolled in the Lubavitcher yeshiva on Allerton Avenue, an Orthodox establishment with strict rules of conduct. It was about a half-hour walk from our apartment, and I was still at the school when my name changed. I was already something of a misfit in the school. When our teacher had previously asked us where we were from, the other students mentioned different neighborhoods in and around New York.

I said, "The Soviet Union."

This was Cold War time at its prime. The other kids were apparently as aghast as they were gleeful, for they all scrawled on the bathroom walls, "Abie is a Commie."

Now I'd have to explain to my classmates that not only was I not a Commie, I wasn't even Abie.

In the fall of 1958, I enrolled in DeWitt Clinton High School as Allan Gerson. I also had a new birthday. Abraham Blumstein was born on July 31, 1944, but Allan Gerson was born on June 19, 1945. My parents and my brother Sam also had their last name changed to Gerson, though Sam got to keep his first name since he was born in Germany and wasn't impersonating anyone else. I never sought any answers. I knew at some level this had to do with my parents' history, but I also knew that those matters we did not discuss. And it didn't really matter all that much; I was tall for my age so I could get away with being in the same class as my contemporaries who were a year older.

DeWitt Clinton High School was my first public school, an all-boys' behemoth that counts James Baldwin, Burt Lancaster, Charles Rangel, Sugar Ray Robinson, and Neil Simon among its many famous alumni. (Girls were admitted in 1983.) I was now in my first secular school, but I carried deeply my identity as a child of Holocaust survivors. In my sophomore year I wrote a term paper for my European History class on the 1943 Warsaw Ghetto Uprising. I have kept it until this day. I described in it how on the day that I completed my research, I walked out of the New York Public Library, and "the tang of Spring was in the air." But suddenly, my notes slipped from my hand, and as I bent to pick them up: "I felt the smell of the burning of human flesh enter my nostrils. I felt the shrill of hysterical screams of some mother whose child has been taken away from her to be deported to some extermination camp…I could no longer view my surroundings as gay and beautiful. As I looked about, my mind kept repeating over and over again, 'This is not a fairy story. This happened in our own time, in our own century of so-called civilization and humanity.' When the word humanity came to my mind, I felt my stomach whine with anger. I wanted, I really wanted to split the blood of my heart on humanity."

My teacher, Mr. Fuchs, gave me an A+ for the paper saying I had "the markings of a true historian" with the only admonition that I could have profited from reading a book by a Polish author he recommended on how the Poles on the other side of the ghetto wall had viewed the uprising.

I graduated from DeWitt Clinton mid-year in January 1962 and was our class valedictorian, though I did not have the highest grades. (The boy with better grades had a stutter, so I was deemed the better speaker.) I initially attended the tuition-free City College of New York, long a bastion for aspiring children of immigrants. I wasn't a great athlete, but I was good enough to wrestle on the freshman team. After that first year, I transferred to the University of Buffalo, which gave me a scholarship and where I won the intramural heavyweight wrestling championship (though I never wrestled on varsity.)

On graduation I attended New York University Law School, and after graduating in 1969, I taught social studies at a special school in Harlem for troubled youths. This enabled me to get a deferment from the military service that often meant a one-way ticket to Vietnam to fight in a war we all detested. A lottery system had been put in place for tying military conscription to the luck of the draw, and I was unlucky. So I took special classes at Hunter College to gain my teaching license, and brushed up on some of the martial arts skills I had acquired over the years. This enabled me to become a Social Studies teacher and in charge of discipline. The latter could be rough: disabling teenagers with knives, protecting others from attack, and generally risking a malicious jolt or two. The job allowed me to do some important work; not insignificantly, it also helped draft deferment. After a year on the job, I decided on another means of deferment.

I had inherited my mom's chronic diastema, a large space between my upper center teeth, which could be cured by orthodontic devices. But once the braces were installed they rendered me, under the Surgeon General's Standards for Fitness for Service in the US Army, disqualified from service because the orthodontic device installed to cure the defect could result in injuries during training.

So, at the age of 25, I was free to do what I wanted. This took me in the direction of international law. In law school I had taken a class on the subject with Prof. Gidon Gottlieb and was sold on it. And so, in 1970, I enrolled in the Hebrew University of Jerusalem Graduate Program for a Masters of Law in International Law. It was a two-year program, and during the second year I took an internship with Israel's Ministry of Justice, which led to one of my more interesting assignments.

The Ministry suspected that KGB agents were infiltrating the country with the wave of new Russian immigrants. It came to our attention that a group of Russian *émigrés* were going to hold a protest at the Western Wall in Jerusalem's Old City; the protest would be over harsh punishments that Russia had meted out against Jewish *refuseniks* and the harsh sentences handed out to a group of Russian Jews who had tried to hijack a Russian plane to take them to Israel. Ministry officials suspected that the leader of the group was a KGB agent. This leader was also an attractive young woman, so when someone senior in the Ministry suggested that I go to the demonstration and try to meet her and determine her true intentions, I cheerfully agreed.

It didn't work out as planned. The Jerusalem Municipality foreign press attaché, whose job was to introduce foreign reporters to the protesters, kept intervening between me and the young woman, so I never found out if she worked for the KGB. But my sojourn was still productive. The name of the attaché was Joan Nathan, and although at the Western Wall we kept getting in each other's way, we happily overcame our differences when she later visited Yale, where I had enrolled in 1972 in its doctoral program. She was escorting Jerusalem's deputy mayor on a speaking tour. We married in 1974 and have raised three amazing children.

It was in Israel as well, through a remarkable coincidence, that I learned more about my true identity.

In pursuing my doctoral dissertation on Israel's administration of the West Bank, I had returned to Israel the following year for research, conducting interviews with most of the mayors of towns and villages on the West Bank. Joan was living in the United States as well, but she was in Israel while I was there, assisting the renowned filmmaker Charles Guggenheim on a documentary. Both of our projects would soon be complicated by the Yom Kippur War. But just prior to its outbreak, we met for brunch at the American Colony Hotel in East Jerusalem. The hotel was a special place: a small, resplendent old Ottoman palace that had been run for generations by a British missionary family and was known as an island of neutrality that welcomed patrons of all faiths and nationalities. All the waiters were Palestinian, and it had a fabulous buffet.

While I was standing in line, I started chatting with an American woman who was then teaching political science at Hebrew University. She said her name was Naomi Kies, and she was standing there with her father, a lawyer from New York. He was an avuncular sort, on the plump side, exuding the confident warmth of a man who had already accomplished all that he had ever sought.

"Hi, I'm Allan," I said, reaching out for his hand.

"Saul Kies," he said, extending his palm.

I blinked as if I couldn't believe what I was hearing. "Saul Kies?" I asked slowly. "Funny, I had an immigration lawyer by that name when I was about thirteen. I even remember his office: on West Forty-Second Street up from Grand Central Station, across Fifth Avenue. First time I had ever been in a lawyer's office."

"Well, I'm an immigration lawyer," he said. "And that's where I had my office. I'm retired now. What did you say your last name is?"

"I didn't. But it's Gerson. I'm Allan Gerson."

Now it was his turn to squint hard as he looked me over. "Allan, don't you remember me?" he asked with a strange look. "Actually, when we met before, you were still little Abe Blumstein."

I froze, as if caught in the crevice of a time warp. I hadn't heard that name, Abe Blumstein, for nearly 15 years, and I had no recollection of this man before me, though I remembered his name, his office, and the diplomas on the wall.

Seeing how stunned I was, Kies picked up the conversation. He said that my parents had hired him to revert their names, and mine and Sam's, to what they had been before we immigrated to the United States. We had used a false name, Blumstein, to gain entry, which is illegal, and Kies had to convince a judge to exonerate my parents for immigration fraud. Kies did so, he told me, by citing "fear of political persecution."

Once the court had granted our family the right to return to our original name—Gerson— someone had to tell me who I really was. According to Kies, he was the one.

"Your father implored me to be the one to tell you on his behalf," he said. "Surely, you remember."

My pulse quickened. Wheels of recollection began to whir as if trying to work their way through the fog of memory. I recalled being ushered into an office with a brass nameplate on a heavy wooden door that read "Saul Kies, Esq., Attorney at Law." Inside, framed diplomas hung on the walls, and subpoenas and briefs, bound in blue covers, some with red ribbons, were stacked on a desk. For all the clarity of that vision, I had zero recall of being told by him or anyone else that the name I had gone by since coming to America— Abraham Blumstein—would be no more, or that, I would be Allan Gerson from then on.

Kies pressed me: "Don't you remember? I congratulated you on now being free to become Bar Mitzvah under your real identity. And since under your new, or original, identity, you had extra time to prepare for your Bar Mitzvah. I knew you were anxious about that."

He explained the deep risks that our family had confronted. We had lied on our entry visa to gain admission under an assumed name; that allowed us to circumvent US quota restrictions, but it also meant that we could face deportation. My parents, according to Kies, had shown true courage in going to court. "It could have gone the other way," he said. "You could have been deported. Don't you remember me telling you that?"

I stared at him blankly. "I don't remember any of it," I said. But I had no doubt that he was telling me the truth. His precise memory of these long-ago events surely reflected his recognition of the potential trauma of the moment: telling a boy he wasn't who he thought he was could have been cataclysmic. And maybe it was. Abraham Blumstein was born on July 31, 1944, while Allan Gerson was born on June 19, 1945. In an instant, I was thirteen months younger. Demoted to being an 11-year-old.

That I was given this news on the cusp of my Bar Mitzvah would have made it all more unnerving—as if my imminent ascent into manhood had been taken away, like a ladder yanked from under my feet.

In time I would learn a bit more about Saul Kies, an immigrant himself who came to America from Latvia in 1922. Active in the Labor Zionist movement, he clearly forged a bond with my parents, who invited him and his wife to my rescheduled Bar Mitzvah in June 1958. In a typewritten written letter that he sent to me, Kies regretfully declined the invitation due to another commitment, but he wrote: "We hope that your Bar Mitzvah will be an important milestone in your growth as a Jew and as an American."

In addition to that letter, my parents kept Kies's invoice for his services: $1,000, in three installments, which was a lot of money for my parents. Reverting our identity to Gerson was clearly important to them, but even after my chance encounter with the lawyer who made it possible, I never asked my parents why. It remained in the "Better Not To Know" box.

Foehrenwald Displaced Persons Camp with Uncle Henik, who survived Auschwitz, and met and married Aunt Ruchsa in the camp, circa 1949.

Chapter Thirteen

Trial and Consequences

Shortly after my parents moved to Miami, Ma met Debby. She was recently widowed, and early every morning they would meet at the large artificial lake at the center of the Point East complex. On my first visit to Point East, I accompanied them for their morning ritual. It was something to observe. They clearly liked each other, and were clearly quite different, at least outwardly. Debby, ten years younger than my mother, was in super shape. She would swim out far, her arms pumping. Ma and I stayed in the shallows. One day, as Debby emerged from the water, exhausted but with a grin of satisfaction, I spotted the uneven tattooed blue numbers on her, indelibly, as a once-prisoner at a Nazi concentration camp.

Later, Ma brought up how much she loved her daily outings with Debby.

"How is she?" I asked, the disparity between her tattooed forearm and the robust woman she now was, still very much on my mind.

"Oh, she's a horse."

"But how does she manage to stay that way?" I asked. "Looking at her you couldn't tell…" My words trailed off.

Ma's reply came shortly thereafter, as if slowly measuring the impact of her words. "She spent three years at Auschwitz, *Ellenu*," she said. "But she wasn't a regular prisoner there. She had…*special privileges*."

"What do you mean?" I asked, still a neophyte in these matters at the time.

Ellenu, Ma sighed, and then spoke slowly: "She played in the orchestra. That big cello you see her lugging around to events here, that's what she played there."

I was beginning to understand. New trainloads of prisoners would arrive. The boxcar doors opened and those who had been packed more tightly than animals spilled out. Terrified, they must have glanced frantically at their new surroundings, at the menacing dogs, and the men with the whips, and perhaps spotting the white pillars of smoke in the distance, coming from the site of the bombed crematoria, drifting up to the sky like funneled summer clouds shaped as pleading palms.

The new arrivals might not yet have had the luxury of unfettered thought. They were undoubtedly already discombobulated by the awful train journey. And now they had the image of the men with the menacing dogs, ready to shred you to pieces to juxtapose with that other incongruous image: the sight of Debby and her fellow musicians, playing Brahms, fugues, and partitas from Bach, and little pieces of Palestrina fluff, lulling them to believing that the thought that they were being ushered to the gas chambers was but a nightmare.

To the gas chambers, against this chorus of classical chamber music? Who could imagine it? But Debby and the others in the orchestra, playing competently, even beautifully, certainly knew what awaited them. Scarlatti for the victims. Mozart for the soon to die. In the cold of winter or under a warm summer sun, white clouds and the silken wisps of the cremated always hovered in the not-so-distant sky, for the knowledgeable a constant reminder of what laid beyond the facade of normalcy.

Truth is, I did not exactly know what Ma meant by the reference to Debby's "special privileges." I had heard whispers that Uncle Henik perhaps had a similar arrangement that accounted for his survival for so many years at Auschwitz. But I had not put two and two together until now. If that was "assistance" to the Nazis, and it certainly looked that way, it could jeopardize their US citizenship, and expose them to deportation in its wake.

The defendants we were charging seemed confident, however, that they had a silver bullet to avoid this outcome. Like the other Nazi collaborators we were soon to confront, Sarowycz had been told by his lawyer not to worry, that American law would never permit—absent a finding that the "assistance" had been voluntarily rendered—deportation in such circumstances. Here, Sarowycz and the others like him in similar positions would have faced a bullet to the back of the head had they not *"assisted"* to assure their own survival. So Sarowycz told us that he had to translate for the Nazis or face being shot. And Osidach was to make the same argument: He had *no choice but to* carry out his responsibilities as police chief (including being in charge of the roundups) or he'd risk being shot. If their conduct constituted *assistance as a matter of fact,* it decidedly did not constitute *assistance as a matter of law.* The law was more merciful and understanding. Free will, acts of knowing commission, were what the law required before meting out punishment.

I had no trouble with that defense. In fact, I welcomed it. It would present us with an opportunity to demonstrate that the defendants were, in fact, *willing executioners,* in the memorable phrase coined by Daniel Goldhagen in his groundbreaking book describing the posture of the German people during the war. For if there was nothing "willing" about the assistance, then what was the point of prosecution? What lesson for future generations? This was especially true as we couldn't shield from our eyes the overwhelming likelihood of the fate of the Ukrainians we were about to deport the USSR: death by firing squad following a sham trial.

Nor did I believe that drawing that fine line between voluntary and involuntary behavior was beyond our ken. Criminal prosecutors in countless courts throughout America are called upon daily to demonstrate *intent* as a precursor to a finding of guilt. Why should less be expected of us in this instance? But the law requires *proximate cause:* the accused's actions must be *causally* related to the injury or death, and I doubted that the judges in America in 1980 could be persuaded that service as a translator for the Nazi SS was a sufficient causal link to the type of "assistance" that warranted denaturalization and deportation. I felt, therefore, that mounting such an effort against Sarowycz, would prove futile. He didn't push anybody onto the trains. He was acting behind the scenes. That was also true of the SS's bankrollers whom Rockler had successfully prosecuted at Nuremberg, but transmitting huge infusions of cash has a more sinister edge than the image of a mild, bespectacled translator.

Osidach was a much easier call. He could not argue that he was little different from a Jewish *kapo* doing what human impulse demanded to survive. He had not, like Fedor Fedorenko, been stuck in a "prisoner of war" camp where the Germans were systematically starving the captured Ukrainian soldiers. Survival was never the issue for Osidach. From the moment that he donned his blue cap and uniform to report to the Nazi command that had taken control of Rawa-Ruska, he surely understood that it was only a matter of time before the Ukrainian auxiliary police under his control would be ordered to round up the Jews, and it was a task that he voluntarily assumed for the cause, as he saw it, of a free Ukraine once the war was over.

In March 1980, Walter Rockler was replaced at OSI by Allan Ryan, who had come on board as a designated director-in-waiting in January. Previously, as a Justice Department attorney in the US Solicitor General's Office, whose caseload is generally confined to cases before the US Supreme Court, he had nevertheless managed to secure permission to represent the government in its successful appeal of the *Fedorenko* case. Ryan saw himself as a prosecutor, not a Nazi hunter, he said in an interview with *The New York Times* about running OSI. "I've never seen this as a Jewish issue," he said. "It should concern everybody. It happened to all of us. But we're not here to avenge the Holocaust. We're here to apply the law."

Ryan approved my recommendation that we bring Osidach to trial, and preparations commenced as several experienced co-counsel—Neal Sher, who had become OSI's deputy director, Rod Smith, and Norm Moscowitz—were added to the case team. Proceeding slowly but methodically, we prepared a brief and several memoranda for the US District Court for the Eastern District of Pennsylvania, sitting in Philadelphia. Specifically, we charged Osidach for unlawfully procuring US citizenship in violation of the 1948 Displaced Persons Act, which deems ineligible for admission any person "to have assisted the enemy in persecuting civil populations."

The trial began in September 1980, and our job was to make *Osidach* our first successful denaturalization and deportation case. It was precisely what I had hoped to accomplish in joining OSI: to show the true face of collaboration as voluntary and in many cases, particularly that of police chiefs like Osidach, politically inspired. His age (76) and infirm health (a heart condition) gave me pause, only in the sense that I wanted to make sure that he was still capable of defending himself, not that he shouldn't be held accountable for his misdeeds.

The night before the trial began, I sat in my hotel room late into the evening, sipping stale black coffee while sifting through a binder of notes. We had documentary evidence of Osidach's many lies on his US visa application. He had written "no" when asked if he had ever been arrested, when in fact he had been arrested repeatedly in Poland for his membership in the Organization of Ukrainian Nationalists (OUN) and had spent six years in prison. He had lied about his affiliation with military organizations during the war, claiming that he had spent those years as a dairy farmer. We had numerous witness statements that identified Osidach as chief of the Ukrainian auxiliary police force in Rawa-Ruska, directly involved in ordering his subordinates to round up the Jews. We also had documentary evidence from the USSR. We had as well four witnesses from the United States, one from France, and two from Israel. But none of them specifically saw Osidach round up the Jews; what they knew of Osidach in that regard was second-hand.

Our most important witness remained Ida, and hopefully she would hold up.

A newspaper clipping hanging halfway out of my briefcase caught my eye. The *Philadelphia Daily News* had reported on the case shortly after we had filed charges against Osidach several months earlier. Under the headline "Alleged Nazi Ally Could Lose Citizenship," the story referred to an exclusive interview that the paper had conducted with Osidach in 1977, when rumors first surfaced about his wartime activities. His response: "These accusations are lies created by the Communists to embarrass me because I have always been anti-Communist ... I had nothing to do with the police."

Passions at the trial were going to run high, as Osidach had the full-throated support of activists in America's Ukrainian community, mainly in New York and Philadelphia, as well as anti-Communists who resented our cooperation with the Soviet Union.

I set down the binder and looked at the clock. Twelve-thirty in the morning. I rubbed my eyes. I needed at least a few good hours of sleep.

The next morning, after a brisk walk to the courthouse with my two co-counsels, Moscowitz and Sher, we entered the courtroom already tense with excitement. The public audience was comprised of roughly even numbers of Jews seeking historic justice and Ukrainian-Americans outraged that one of their countrymen might be deported with the assistance of the Soviet Union.

I sat next to Norm, and as we awaited the judge's arrival—this was a non-jury trial—we passed around the appendix of the 52 exhibits.

Osidach's legal defense team consisted of one rumpled solo practitioner, Louis Konowal. He was clearly outmatched. In his answers to the government's submissions before the trial, he filed documents filled with typos and poorly reasoned arguments, often veering into diatribes. He wrote to the court: "The defendant suggests that the inclusion in by the United States in its Complaint and Affidavit of an alleged persecutions, crimes and murders is impertinent, scandalous, and libellouis (sic) and should be stricken by the United States on its own Motions and Amended Pleadings filed omitting all reference to any crimes or criminal conduct."

Konowal entered the courtroom, followed by an unsteady-looking Osidach and his wife, Ivanne. Osidach was nearly bald, his complexion a pasty off-white. Ivanne, who was 63, was also pale, her hair disheveled. He seemed to be wearing hearing aids behind his thick dark eyeglass frames. Both looked shell-shocked. Judge Louis Bechtle had ordered that a nurse be present throughout the trial, whether Osidach was on or off the stand, at government expense. (Osidach's doctor had written to the court warning of the dangers to his patient in a high-profile trial.) Ivanne helped him sit down next to the nurse, who adjusted the mobile oxygen supply to his nose.

The three sat across from us at a table separating plaintiffs from defendants, and the trial began. Because they had more courtroom experience, Moscowitz and Sher questioned all the witnesses, and one of our most important was Raul Hilberg, a historian who was the world's leading expert on the Holocaust. Born in Austria in 1926, he had watched the ascendance of Nazism up close—after the Nazis had annexed Austria in 1938, his family was evicted from their home. His father was also arrested but then released, because of his military service in the First World War. Raul's family fled Austria, passed through France, and embarked on a ship to America, arriving on September 1, 1939, the first day of the war. Twenty-six members of Raul's family died in the Holocaust, and that motivated him to document the annihilation in its entirety. He examined every German record and military order that found its way into the Allied archives, especially those he worked on while assigned to the US Army's War Documentation Project in 1948. He amassed, sorted, and synthesized the grisly details on the complex machinery of genocide: its preparation, implementation, and near-completion. All of this was incorporated in his master work, *The Destruction of the European Jews*, published in 1961, a staggering three-volume study in lucid, unsparing prose across nearly 1,400 pages.

Hilberg was OSI's expert witness on a number of our early cases, and he had become a personal friend during his many visits to Washington. Once, we took a walk along 14th Street's seedy corridor outside our offices, and I told him about my family history, posing the question that I was eager to ask. I felt like the long-distance sojourner who had reached the top of a fabled mountain to inquire of a wise man the secret of the universe.

"Professor Hilberg," I asked, "can you tell me, after all your thinking on the subject, why did the Germans do what they did? I mean, I understand Hitler as someone deranged who had a coterie of slavish followers, but why did he cut such a wide swath, gather so much popular support, genuine enough, across all of Germany with Germans from all walks of life, including the military professionals, in the craze to kill as many Jews as they could find wherever they could find them?"

It was a long-winded question, to which he gave a very short answer:

"I only studied the *how*," he said. "I never understood the *why*."

His comment echoed Primo Levi's conversation with the Auschwitz guard: *Here, there is no why.*

At the trial, Hilberg testified definitively about the *how*. Based on his exhaustive review of thousands of documents in various depositories around the world, he testified that it was beyond doubt that in the eastern part of pre-war Poland (Galicia), large numbers of Ukrainians were used in SS combat battalions and deployed at death camps and in ghettoes, including in the Warsaw Ghetto Uprising. In particular, he said, the Ukrainian police were regularly used to deport Jews, and Ukrainian guards constituted the bulk of those who ran the extermination camps.

On cross-examination, he was asked about the particular role of Ukrainian police in Rawa-Ruska. "It would have been inconceivable," he said, "for the Ukrainian police in Rawa-Ruska *not* to have been involved in the roundups of Jews, for such collaboration was the pattern throughout Galicia."

To blunt the impact of that testimony, Konowal called to the stand Dr. Petro Mirchuk, who was described as an expert on Ukrainian nationalism and the Organization of Ukrainian Nationalists. Mirchuk testified that the Ukrainian police were not involved in acts of persecution against Jews throughout Galicia, including in Rawa-Ruska. But on cross-examination, he acknowledged that he had not undertaken any independent research on the murder of the Jews of eastern Poland and Ukraine in the early 1940s, and that his testimony was based solely on his general knowledge.

The trial's most important witness, of course, was Osidach, and he took the stand with the oxygen tube attached to his nose. He responded to Neal's questions in a voice that often quivered, and at times he seemed to shrink in the chair. His English was choppy. He testified that he resided in Rawa-Ruska from January 1942 until the summer of 1944, when the Nazi occupation ended, and he said that as the police chief, he served as a translator for the Germans. He confirmed that he wore a dark blue uniform and a badge and carried a pistol, and he described what he knew of the Jewish ghetto, which was sealed off by a fence and wire. Though he had never gone into the ghetto, "I know the conditions were bad," he said. "Jewish people used to go secretly out from the ghetto to get some food."

"And it was from these people," Neal asked, "that you learned what the conditions were like in ghetto?"

"From these people."

"You learned that the conditions were very crowded in the ghetto?"

"One can see that in every step."

Osidach said that the Jews suffered from health problems, such as typhus, and also from starvation, but they were not allowed to leave the ghetto by themselves. When they did leave, they were easy to identify because they wore yellow armbands with the Star of David.

Neal asked if he ever saw the Jews being taken to the railroad station.

"I saw," Osidach said.

"And you saw this very often?"

"I can't say it has been every day, but from time to time, I saw it."

Neal showed him a deposition in which he said he saw Jews being taken "very often."

Was it very often?

"No," Osidach said. "I'm saying 'often.' That is all."

Osidach said he saw large groups being taken to the train station used for cattle and "other manufacturer," but he did not see how the Jews were loaded.

Neal asked him: "Now, in these large groups of Jews marching toward the railroad station, were there women?"

"There were."

"Were there men?"

"There were."

"Were there children?"

"There were."

"These Jews were guarded as they were taken to the railroad station, is that right?"

"Yes, they were."

"Who guarded them, Mr. Osidach?"

"The German defense police, the gendarmes, and basically the Gestapo, the SS."

Osidach said that neither he nor any Ukrainian police guarded the Jews or rounded them up. He only kept order in the stores, he said, not the streets. Asked if he knew that the Jews were being sent to Belzec, Osidach said he had heard the Jews were being sent to "some camp," but he had not seen it, and "the Germans had many camps."

If Osidach didn't know what happened at the death camps, he knew happened in Rawa-Ruska, and Neal wanted him to speak to that.

"Do you recall shootings in the ghetto?" Neal asked.

"Sometimes I heard some shooting."

"And did you see fire in the ghetto?"

"Only when they were liquidating the ghetto."

"The ghetto was liquidated in the winter of 1942-43, is that right?"

"Probably."

Osidach said he heard explosions.

"You heard explosions of bombs?" Neal asked.

"Maybe dynamite."

"Dynamite?"

"Dynamite and fire."

"Did you hear screaming?"

"There was such an explosion, I wasn't very close. That time was burning almost the whole city."

"How long did the final liquidation last?"

"It lasted a long time," Osidach said. "I can't recall exactly, but I presume more than a week."

Neal asked about Osidach's entry into the United States in 1949. He pulled out the defendant's official INS file and retrieved a so-called IRO Resettlement Form, which required Osidach to identify his employment history for the 12 years prior to his immigration. From May 1944 to 1949, the form said that Osidach was variously an autoworker and a secretary in Germany, but during his years in Nazi-occupied Rawa-Ruska, the document said he worked for a dairy association as a "dairy technic."

Neal: "You were not a dairy technic for all of 1942, were you, Mr. Osidach?"

"No."

"And you were not a dairy technic in 1944, were you?"

"No."

"As a matter of fact, Mr. Osidach, during those years, you were a Ukrainian policeman."

"Yes."

Osidach acknowledged lying on his immigration form, which was essential for a determination of fraudulent entry, and at the end of two long days of testimony—about yellow armbands and trains heading to oblivion and the immolation of a ghetto—Wolodymir Osidach and his oxygen tank stepped down from the stand.

OSI's collaboration with the Soviet Union was the price we paid to prosecute the case. We needed records from Poland, and the Soviet Union's control of that country gave us access to documents there as well as in Moscow. We realized that in using such evidence, the government was helping the Soviets intimidate Ukrainian and Baltic Republic nationalists in the US, some of whom might now be deported for crimes long ago. But for OSI, the price was worth it. In the Osidach case alone, thanks to the Soviets, we amassed his immigration records, his Polish arrest and employment records, academic works on Nazi-occupied Rawa-Ruska, and mounds of grainy black-and-white photos. All documents were approved by Judge Bechtle, as were the videotaped depositions of Russian witnesses.

Our cooperation with the Soviets, however, stirred bitter controversy, and not just with the Ukrainian-American community. Hard-line anti-Communists also denounced us, none more than Patrick Buchanan. A pugnacious former speechwriter for President Nixon who would have that same role for President Reagan, Buchanan used his perch as newspaper and television commentator to attack OSI in its case against Osidach and other suspected Nazi collaborators. It was "Orwellian and Kafkaesque," Buchanan wrote about our efforts against one such suspect, "to deport an American citizen to the Soviet Union to stand trial for collaboration with Adolph Hitler when the principal collaborator with Hitler in starting World War II was that self-same Soviet government."

Given the Soviets' cruelty toward my parents, I was the last person to want to see them gain an upper hand, but I agreed that we needed to work with them; we needed their cooperation. The arrangement gave OSI the opportunity to document how few Germans were needed for the task of extermination precisely because so many collaborators stood ready to be of service.

Ida took the stand after Osidach and was questioned by Norm Moscowitz. While she was hardly a robust figure, her answers were straightforward and compelling. Norm asked her what kind of work her husband did after the Nazis took over Rawa-Ruska.

Ida said that he and others dug ditches.

"How long did they do this work?" Norm asked.

"Very short. They took away the whole group."

"And what happened to them?"

"They never came back."

Norm asked if she remembered when Bert and I had met with her at her home in January and had asked her to identify someone in a photo spread.

Ida said she did remember, noting that the person in question "arrested my brother." She herself was arrested, she said, when she left the ghetto to find bread and was approached by a Ukrainian guard, who said to her, "You lived enough. Now you are going with me."

When she reached the train station, she said, she recognized the guards and even knew them personally.

"They were from the Baron Hirsch School," she said. "That was their station."

Her testimony squarely rebutted Osidach's claims that only the Germans, not the Ukrainians, rounded up the Jews.

Ida offered a shortened version of how she survived by jumping off the moving train, as that part of her life story was of little interest to the court. What mattered was what she knew of the defendant.

"Where did you last see Mr. Osidach?" Norm asked.

"I saw him when he arrested—when he escorted my brother to the court," she said.

"This is in which city?"

"In Rawa-Ruska. It was summer ... I came out ... and I saw that my brother was in front, and [Osidach] was in the back with his rifle."

She said she was afraid that if she got too close, she too would be arrested. Norm asked what happened to her brother.

"They took him to the courthouse in Rawa-Ruska, and that was that."

"What was Mr. Osidach wearing at the time?"

"His rifle and his uniform."

"What color was his uniform?"

"I think maybe blue or something, yes."

"And what was the closest you were to him at this time that you saw him?"

"How close was I? I was very close, only I ran away."

"Did you look at Osidach's face then?"

"Oh, yes. He saw me too."

In response to a question from Judge Bechtle, Ida estimated that she was eight to 10 feet from Osidach.

"Was it day or night?" the judge asked.

"Day, a summer day. A beautiful nice day."

"How long did you see him for?"

"Maybe a quarter of an hour."

"Fifteen minutes?"

"Fifteen minutes."

Her testimony was clear and specific, and Konowal's cross-examination did little to dent her story and in fact only made Ida stronger. After a series of aimless questions about the photo spread, Ida snapped, "I will tell you one thing. I was working my life, years and years for a lawyer in Poland, and I never, never hear such a thing like you are asking me!"

The courtroom erupted in snickers.

Otherwise, Ida displayed little anger or resentment on the stand, toward Osidach or anyone else. Indeed, her testimony revealed the connections between her and her persecutors. Asked by Norm if she had ever met Osidach before, Ida said she had met him before the war. "I was walking in the street, and I was with a friend of mine, Ingenia Lubivitski … and my friend introduced him to me. 'Hello, how are you?' And he passed me by, and that was all I saw of him."

"Never spoke to him again?"

"No, never."

"Did you know anyone else in Mr. Osidach's family?"

"I knew his wife when she was a small girl."

"What is her name?"

"Ivanne Bozyk."

"Did you know anyone else in her family?"

"Her sister went to school with me, and I knew her father."

"What was her sister's name?"

"Olga Terpeluk."

Her tone did not convey whether she was talking about maniacal men who tried to kill her or childhood acquaintances with whom she lost touch.

I understood that ambivalence.

At some point in the trial, Norm turned to me. "Allan, how does it feel, sitting so close, practically on the same bench, as Osidach?"

The question took me by surprise, as did my answer. "I feel nothing, nothing at all," I said.

Norm looked at me suspiciously.

"Nothing at all," I repeated.

But I did feel something, something I could barely articulate then. It was a sensation, akin to an acute sense of hollowness. I felt like crying, precisely because I felt nothing. It was as if I was robbed of the luxury of my own hate.

Perhaps it was because Osidach was dependent on oxygen tanks and a nurse and seemed mystified by the judge in his black robe and the documents on the table and the audience benches filled with partisans who would occasionally scream out something in protest. Perhaps it would have been different if it were Sarowycz who was sitting there, healthy and cunning, instead of a retired slaughterhouse worker from Philadelphia. Or perhaps it had nothing to do with the person on trial but the trial itself that seemed so far removed from reality, an artificial construct. For this was no longer 1947 and the Nuremberg War Crimes Tribunal. This was 1980. And so, what should have been a moment of vindication was a moment of hollowness because nothing we could do here was visceral any longer. There were no more Jews to be protected, except in the most theoretical jurisprudential sense.

It was like the case we studied in law school about the cannibals on the British shipwreck: those who survived on a raft decided after ten days with no food or water to drown the young boy with them and eat him so they could survive. When this was later discovered and they were brought to trial for murder, the judge could not say that faced with similar circumstances he or anybody else would not have done the same, but he nevertheless had to sentence them to the gallows so that it would be an object lesson to others. Is that what this trial was about? And who would draw that lesson? Meanwhile, if Osidach were deported to a Soviet-controlled territory, he would be prosecuted as a traitor, and real flesh would be torn and real blood spilled.

I drew solace from a conversation I had with one of the Israeli witnesses who had come to Philadelphia to testify. He had seen Osidach as police chief but he had escaped Rawa-Ruska before the roundups began. At one point, I turned to him and asked how he felt confronting Osidach in person.

"It's too many years after the event to feel anything," he said. "The anger has seeped out of me like squeezed lemons; too many tears have left me dry."

"So why did you come to testify?" I asked.

"For my children and my grandchildren," he answered. "I want the world to know what those Ukrainians did in Rawa-Ruska, in destroying our lives, in obliterating Jewish life. The Germans planned it, the Ukrainians did it. I want everyone to know. But—"

he leaned over to confide in me. "During the recess, I had to go to the bathroom, and so did he, and he stood next to me at the urinal. We were both standing, old men holding on to our limp penises as we peed. I think he finished first, and then I held the door for him as we went out. What was I supposed to do? Spit in his face? The face doesn't even any longer look the same."

After nearly two weeks, in which we put 14 in-court witnesses on the stand, Judge Bechtle determined that Osidach was too ill to continue. Even the prosecution had reached the same conclusion, as we saw him wheeze and gasp for air on the witness stand, especially each time we produced another Soviet document corroborating the government's case. Judge Bechtle announced that he would excuse Osidach from ever having to be in the courtroom again, and the remainder of the trial would be conducted via filings from both parties. When that was over, he would render his decision.

My colleagues were confident of victory, and leaving the court, they wanted to celebrate over a few beers. I told them I'd join them later, and after a brisk walk down Market Street, I got to my hotel room, plopped down on my bed, and almost mechanically began sifting through my notes. Catching my attention was Exhibit 25, a military memo from a German intelligence officer from November 1942, on the mentality of the Jews ensnared in roundups. Noting that "Jews have been quartered on a large scale in camps erected by the SS," the memo said that these measures have a "crushing effect on the psychic and hence also physical condition of the Jews," who come to believe that their families will soon be victims. That assumption will be proven right, the memo said, during "a major resettlement action which is in store for Lviv in the next few days."

I had highlighted the exhibit for my own reference, even though it said nothing directly about Rawa-Ruska. Still, I had wanted this note as a reminder—a reminder that had my mother and father stayed in Lviv and had they not been deported to Siberia, they would have been rounded up and sent to Belzec soon thereafter. I already knew that, of course. But seeing it in print, in the words of German intelligence officer, was still jarring.

After the Germans took control of Lviv in 1941, the Jews placed in its ghetto reached 220,000, and those who did not quickly succumb to mass shootings, forced labor, or starvation were dispatched on narrow railroad trestles bound for either Belzec or the smaller killing field at Janowska. As documented, the SS ordered these actions, and the Ukrainian police helped carry them out through the same kind of units that Osidach commanded. By June 1943, there would be nothing left of the Lviv ghetto.

I looked at another document, Exhibit 26. It was a report by a German non-commissioned officer, Wilhelm Cornides, recording his impressions of events. "Many trainloads of Jews from Lviv passed Rawa-Ruska on the way to Belzec. After Auschwitz and Treblinka, it is our most important extermination camp. Its location is along a well-travelled railroad line linking Zamość, Rawa-Ruska, and Lviv."

There was no need to refer to this exhibit at the trial, but for me it completed the picture: Zamość, Rawa-Ruska, and Lviv were all sides of one triangle set against the savagery of a place named Belzec, equidistant from all three.

Looking over these documents was proof that I had made it into life by a whisker. One different move, one note of hesitation on my parents' part, and their fate like the others would have been sealed. It was a coincidence—or, dare I say, was there a divine Hand in it— that this was my first OSI case. Perhaps, I allowed myself to think, some mystical hand was at work so that out of the silence of the years, I would have Aunt Raya's photos to guide me and Saul Kies to tell me what my father never had: that I am his son, a Gerson, not a Blumstein, my old name and age now sealed, so that the boy who I was is no more, my identity effaced by an American judge I never met, but now standing before another American judge to speak of the awful triangle that linked Rawa-Ruska, Zamość and Lviv to the trains bound for Belzec with their loads of hapless Jews rounded up, at least in part, by the likes of Osidach and his auxiliary police.

And perhaps, too, it occurred to me, this is what I was called upon to do in 1979 by joining OSI: to ensure that the true identities of the others, the tormentors, were never effaced, but recorded for all time. *That* would be the reward. Perhaps deportation was something custom-made for those with stronger constitutions, not for someone like myself, whose parents had lied to enter the United States and then lived in fear of deportation. But I had my role to play. Of this I was sure: that I was meant to at least create an irrefutable record.

In March 1981, Judge Bechtle ruled that Osidach had lied about his participation in assisting the Nazis, asserting that he was "a necessary link between the Germans and the objects of their persecutions—the Jews in the town of Rawa-Ruska." The judge ordered Osidach to be denaturalized, and the government would then move to deport him.

Two months later, before any appeal could be heard or a deportation hearing could be held, Wolodymir Osidach died. His heart had given out.

Allan Gerson with his daughter, Daniela, Uncle Henik, and Aunt Ruchsa in the Bronx, 1981.

Chapter Fourteen

Civiletti's Argument

I was already nervous about the case involving Feodor Fedorenko, the Ukrainian truck driver who had served as a guard in Treblinka, immigrated to America, and was then charged for concealing his wartime activities and lying on his visa application. I thought the government should have honed in on whether his actions as a guard had been willful and voluntary, and that question alone—his *mens rea*, his criminal intent. But government prosecutors as well as the Court of Appeals focused on whether the misleading visa application *might* have led to denial, after it *might* have precipitated an investigation, had it been truthful. And concluding that this *might have occurred*, the Court gave the government wide prosecutorial discretion in pursuing immigration fraud.

Now the US Supreme Court was going to review the case, with arguments on October 15, 1980. I was not directly involved in it, but I was keenly interested. Like the *Osidach* case, it would set a precedent for the rest of OSI's work, and it also threw into sharp relief the most important questions surrounding our mission: How do we assess individual guilt under extreme circumstances? What constitutes voluntary or involuntary actions in a death camp? How is justice dispensed after all these years?

I tried to make my view clear: that this should not be a matter of OSI prevailing technically by whatever leeway the law provided; that our tactics had to be tied to an overall objective; and that overall objective should be creating a record of *willing* collaboration. Only by establishing that the defendant's actions were voluntary, and creating a historical record thereof, could we morally justify stripping Fedorenko's citizenship and deporting him.

But my colleagues didn't see it that way. They believed in the Irish statesman and philosopher Edmund Burke's famous maxim, "The law sharpens the mind by narrowing it." But they saw that narrowing as a virtue, not as a vice—the warning Burke had intended. As applied to his case, it meant narrowing our focus to Fedorenko's "assistance" without regard to the broader, and more significant, question of whether he had willingly collaborated. That would have meant proving state of mind, and that was deemed too difficult, and in any event, not explicitly called for by Congress in the enabling legislation, the DP Act of 1948.

I was also troubled by a couple of other questions. First, why among the thousands of cases the US Supreme Court is implored to review each year, did it choose this particular one, of limited applicability—ostensibly pertaining only to victims of the Holocaust? To be sure, the Supreme Court presides where ordinary mortals will not dare to tread, responsible only to itself to explain its choice of cases to review. Still, there is a logic to the method. It usually chooses to rule on cases that are of national significance and on which it wants to make a statement. Perhaps the Court surmised that this case was, after all, about something larger than the fate of Fedorenko, something larger than the cause of historic justice affecting Nazi cohorts and Jewish victims, something that went wider, to the very essence of US immigration policy. Perhaps that was why it chose this particular case.

Second, US Attorney General Benjamin Civiletti was to be arguing for the government. It would be the only argument that he presented to the Supreme Court during his tenure as attorney general. He did this in part, I assumed, because the record was relatively small and could be mastered in short order.

I dutifully took my seat on the bench nearest to Civiletti. Sitting next to him were OSI head Allan Ryan and Solicitor General Wade McCree.

At 9 a.m. on the dot, the Court's nine justices entered the chamber, magisterial black robes flowing to their feet as they seated themselves in their imposing large black leather chairs. As they prepared to call the hearing to order, they conferred briefly among themselves. This was my first appearance before the US Supreme Court; although not arguing the case, I was part of the government team. I had already argued cases in almost every US court of appeals. But the Supreme Court, in its stark majesty, and its nine justices peering down at you from on high, was an entirely different experience. My focus was not, however, on the justices, but on Attorney General Civiletti. I was specifically focused on how broadly or narrowly he would choose to fashion his argument when responding to the questions that were to soon bombard him.

Two years earlier, the justices had installed a secret recording system. Although the Court had experimented with various recording systems since the 1950s, few Americans knew that the Supreme Court had recently installed an updated secret recording system for the justices' own use. It is no longer in effect, apparently dismembered in 1981. But for court proceedings in 1980, you can actually go to the US National Archives and listen to the justices, their voices captured by a microphone so acute that it picked up banter among the justices that was clearly intended for their ears only. Why the justices felt they needed such a recording remains a mystery, as court stenographers are fully adept at accurately transcribing oral arguments. Perhaps it had been intended as a fail-safe in case there were ever any potential high-stakes cases for which they wanted to review their bench exchanges. Either way, a voice recording of the *Fedorenko* hearing remains available to the public, and it is revealing.

For example, there is this six-second remark:

Justice Harry Blackmun, probably to Chief Justice Warren Burger, who sat to his left: "Today I bet [Civiletti] wishes we televised arguments, so he could be on the 6 o'clock news and impress the Jews."

Justice Blackmun might have been merely expressing his displeasure that Civiletti supported camera coverage of appellate court proceedings. Still, the comment is not reassuring. Why would the chief justice and a senior justice like Blackmun believe that the US attorney general would be so intent on using court hearings to "impress the Jews?"

Maybe the justices view all of their cases through a political lens, and they saw this one as a way for the Carter administration, on the eve of a presidential election, to curry favor with Jewish voters. Or maybe Justice Blackmun did, in fact, harbor an ill-defined anti-Jewish bias.

But if Civiletti's appearance had been calculated to bolster the

Jewish vote, his actual argument had less to do with fulfilling any sense of historic justice to the Jewish community than it had to do with how the courts should interpret US immigration laws—an interpretation that could endanger the citizenship of any US citizen who had lied on his or her forms for whatever reason and under whatever circumstances to gain entry.

Fedorenko's lawyer, Brian M. Gildea of New Haven, Connecticut, spoke first. His opening statement was surprisingly weak. He began by characterizing at length what he deemed the central issue before the Court: whether the Fifth Circuit had misconstrued the meaning of "material misrepresentation" as it relates to immigration. As defined by US law, it encompassed any distortion of the truth that, if revealed, would have mandated denial of entry.

But the Court surely knew the issues surrounding this matter, and a one-sentence recitation would have sufficed.

Justice Potter Stewart, growing impatient, interrupted Gildea's presentation in an effort to get straight to the heart of the matter.

"Counsel," Justice Stewart asked, "just as a matter of practical information, if Mr. Fedorenko loses this review, what happens to him? Is he deportable?"

There was no mistaking that this was a gift, a good-natured prompt for Fedorenko's attorney to do what good attorneys do on behalf of their clients, even in the rarefied atmosphere of a Supreme Court hearing: show that all hell and brimstone—"irreparable harm" in legalese—would descend from the heavens if the Court failed to do what the attorney was urging. Specifically, Fedorenko would be stripped of his US citizenship. In addition to the stigma attached to denaturalization, deportation proceedings would nearly invariably follow, and deporting Fedorenko to the Soviet Union was a sure-fire ticket to a firing squad.

But if Stewart's softball question invited Gildea to address the grim reality of what Fedorenko faced were the Court to rule against him, Gildea seemed oblivious to what he was being invited to do.

"Your Honor," Gildea responded without an ounce of emotion, "if his citizenship is taken away, he would be subject to further proceedings under the Deportation Section of the Immigration and Nationality Act. At this point, he simply loses his citizenship, if the Supreme Court holds that the appellate court was correct."

Simply loses his citizenship? Given the circumstances, where

Soviet authorities would await Fedorenko's arrival not with vodka and caviar but with a quick trial for treason, denaturalization meant a lot more than a simple loss of citizenship. Gildea failed to pick up on the prompt to paint a panoply of horrors, a vision of heartbreak culminating in a tragic end for an old man, should the Court rule against him. Instead, the lawyer continued to dwell on the complexities of the law that militated in favor of reversing the Fifth Circuit ruling and restoring a lower court's decision to block deportation.

But, after several more minutes, Gildea found his voice. He pointed out that it was the Jews themselves who were bound to suffer most if the Fifth Circuit's ruling was not reversed. He warned that if the Supreme Court ruled that voluntariness—or willful actions—was irrelevant in determining the guilt or innocence of those who assisted the Nazis, then Jewish death camp survivors could now find their US citizenship at risk. As his argument gathered steam, some of the justices began stirring uneasily.

Gildea by then must have felt that he was at last having an impact, for his stride quickened. Fedorenko "was starved, he was beaten, and he was forced to work or die," Gildea said, "and only because he chose not to die, did he allow himself to be trained to serve as a guard, and was given a uniform, boots, and trained to operate and handle a weapon. That was a rifle. He was then sent to the Treblinka Camp, where he served involuntarily as a guard for 10 months...but only as a perimeter guard, and had nothing to do with the actual operation of the gas chambers."

Gildea made no mention that Fedorenko had enjoyed weekly, unescorted furloughs to a neighboring village that accorded him opportunities to escape. It was hard to believe that Gildea was unaware of this fact. He just chose, as lawyers do, to fudge the truth, or skirt it. Little surprise, as the truth would be a reminder that what Fedorenko did, he did voluntarily and willfully. Disregard Fedorenko's furloughs and his soldier's duty to attempt escape if at all possible, and Fedorenko's story had all the tear-jerk quality of a man who was compelled to act as he did.

But those contravening facts couldn't be ignored; they were part of the record. So, too was the fact that the US Army Field Manual, like the Soviet Union's, does not countenance a captured soldier's acquiescence to becoming an armed guard in the enemy's prison compound. Nor does it matter if he was just a "perimeter" guard, not if he had any chance of escape. An American soldier who made such a decision would face a lengthy prison sentence. A Soviet soldier would face execution.

As Gildea pressed his argument that Fedorenko was merely "a perimeter guard." doing what anyone would have done under the circumstances to survive, it was hard to detect any sign of sympathy from any of the Justices. Yet it's a fool's errand to predict which way judges are likely to rule based on their questions, and even less so on their facial expressions. I can recall too many appellate arguments where I thought that a judge was favorably disposed to what I had to say, only later to discover otherwise.

Gildea moved to his next point. Prosecutorial discretion was an invitation to abuse. If, he warned, any misstatement, however innocent, on a visa application could be deemed a "material misrepresentation" for purposes of denaturalization, then government prosecutors would be vested with unchecked power to strip American immigrants of their US citizenship.

The argument was a good one, capable of resonating well with both liberal and conservative Justices. But unfortunately for Gildea, he had run out of his allotted thirty minutes, having expended too much time on an overly long recitation of the facts. The little red light on his podium was flashing. He had no choice but to gather his papers and return to his seat.

Civiletti now rose to the lectern. "Mr. Chief Justice," he said, addressing Justice Burger, "and may it please the Court: Although the facts in this case stretch back 10 years, 35 years, those facts, and the issues presented in this case, have been relevant throughout that time, are important today, and I suggest are important for the future." By 10 years he was presumably referring to when Fedorenko came to the attention of the US government, and by 35 years, to the end of the war.

A promising beginning, I thought. He's going to focus on misrepresentations that involve crimes against humanity and atrocities. My optimism was premature. In the next sentence, he changed tack.

At issue in this case, he argued, is the "entire operation of questions dealing with entry, resident alien-ship status, and denaturalization as well as deportation."

Civiletti's intent was clear enough. He was urging the Supreme Court to not view the *Fedorenko* case as it centers on the accountability of Nazi collaborators. Rather, he urged that the Court take the bold step of using the case as a vehicle to fashion broad standards for strict enforcement of all US immigration laws. Gildea had specifically warned that such a ruling could implicate any number of Jewish Holocaust survivors who did what they had to in order to survive by engaging in some form of "assistance" and who then entered the United States through some sort of falsehood—of material misrepresentation—but Civiletti seemed content to brush that concern aside.

Indeed, Civiletti was arguing that the circumstances of the lying to US immigration officials, of the misrepresentation, are irrelevant: whether occurring under duress or not, a lie is a lie, though the government, he said, in its discretion, would not pursue Jewish victims.

To my dismay, Civiletti did not dwell on the fact that Fedorenko had ample opportunity to stop collaborating with the Nazis, as escape was a reasonable possibility. What Fedorenko specifically did in Treblinka, his actions in assisting with the murders, was now secondary to the semantics of immigration law which, Civiletti contended, "allows the government to prove materiality by showing that the facts, if known, would have been useful in an investigation which might discover grounds or facts warranting a denial of citizenship."

That approach seemed to be conferring nearly unbridled discretion on the government, as the word "might" is open-ended, subject to exploitation at will.

I wasn't the only one who was struck by that formulation for yanking US citizenship. Justice Brennan raised this concern: "As I understand the government's position, it is not that the government has to prove that the investigation would have turned up facts that would have required the denial of citizenship, but rather that it *might* have required a denial of citizenship after an investigation."

Civiletti responded without qualification: "That's exactly right, Justice Brennan."

At that point my stomach felt sick.

Another justice, unidentified in the transcript of the hearing, joined in. "Is there a statutory authority for denaturalizing a person on the grounds that even though his application was completely true, there was at the time of the application a fact in existence which if known would have disqualified him?"

Now, things were really getting out of control, as the question conferred endless discretion to federal prosecutors to strip US citizenship. For even if the visa application "was completely true," it could nevertheless serve as the basis for revoking citizenship if facts were in existence that the applicant was not aware of at the time. This was a hypothetical question, as it assumed facts beyond those presented in the *Fedorenko* case, and Civiletti could have simply said that and deferred answering the question.

Instead, he said, "I think so, yes."

Adding further concern, another unidentified Justice asked: "But there's no statute of limitations on the right to denaturalize?"

Civiletti: "There is no statute of limitations on the right to denaturalize; that's correct." Of course, in most criminal proceedings, even for murder, let alone lesser offenses, most states provide a statute of limitations for bringing a prosecution many years after the event.

Finally, in the last segment of the government's presentation, the issue turned squarely to misrepresentation of a fact that on its face did not deal with covering up the commission of a heinous act or war crime but merely involved a technical deficiency—for example, circumventing stricter eligibility for entry rules, as had been the case with my parents. The numbers had simply tightened for Jewish DPs seeking entry into America, so they represented themselves as a couple that had legitimately obtained a visa to the United States.

Could that person, Justice Stevens asked, decades after he had established himself in the United States, now be subjected to having his citizenship stripped and then be deported?

Justice Stevens: "Supposing for example that, at the time he applied for a visa, they were only issuing visas to college graduates or married persons or something like that, and he concealed his marital status or his educational status, and therefore got a visa, then came over and lived here for twenty or thirty years, and then filed the same kind of application for naturalization that [Fedorenko] did here. Would the government be entitled to denaturalize that person?"

Civiletti: "I think the answer to that question is the government feels that fraud conducted at that time [is serious] ... we can reach back and denaturalize him for that fraud."

No consideration would be given for the passage of time, for the planting of roots, for the Americanization of one's children. None of this would militate against the government's discretion to deport at will. I recognized that such a posture would make it easier to punish Nazi enablers without the messy business of divining the perpetrator's state of mind. But it would come at a painful price, both to Holocaust survivors and to other immigrants who, for whatever reasons, were less than truthful on their entry papers. For Holocaust survivors, it meant that they could never be assured of a complete record establishing that their tormentors were *willing* executioners. For other immigrants who would be in violation, they faced deportation so many years after they had made a new life here only to come up against the lies of long ago, for which they would not even be accorded the right of an explanation.

As made evident in Civiletti's response to Justice Stevens' questioning, he could have as easily been talking about Mexican immigrants as he was about Nazi henchmen. In fact, I was beginning to wonder if his responses weren't more directly focused on them as he emphasized the government's objective of strict enforcement of US immigration laws across the board.

My brain was awash with conflicting impulses: I was refuting the government's case even while working for the government, and I was seeing things from the vantage point of the illegal immigrant, fused with the perspective of the Holocaust survivor's son for whom revenge had passed and what mattered most was a record of willful collaboration.

Chief Justice Burger closed the hearing. "Thank you, gentlemen," he said. "The case is submitted."

There was nothing left to do but head back to our respective offices and await the Court's decision. Outside, on the Court's marble steps, reporters had gathered to interview Civiletti, but he eluded them, heading straight to the black limousine waiting at curbside to return him to the Justice Department. Gildea carried on his argument for any reporters wishing to take note that involuntary conduct could never be a legitimate basis for deportation and that he expected the Supreme Court's ruling to say no less.

Ryan jumped into a car taking him back to OSI. I decided to walk. My mind swirled with thoughts of how the ruling might affect immigrants beyond Fedorenko, including Molly and Uncle Henik, and perhaps even my own parents, not to mention the undocumented immigrants who were maids and chauffeurs to Washington's powerful and whose children were making their way through the US educational system. The only thing that was clear was that my time at OSI was on a short leash. I didn't have the same relationship with Ryan that I had with Rockler. I had been left out of an important research trip to Moscow and did not have the same standing in the office that I'd had previously. More important, I thought the mission itself had begun to veer from what I had imagined it to be, or maybe I had veered from what I'd thought my own mission was. There were too many contradictions to reconcile.

Allan Gerson with Family in the Bronx, 1970.

Chapter Fifteen

Like Actors on a Stage

If the Supreme Court were to rule as Civiletti had urged—considering only the lies themselves rather than whether the acts being covered up had been voluntary—the fallout could be wide indeed. Would the INS suddenly come after Uncle Henik? I had to chuckle at the thought of how he might respond to such an impertinent inquiry by a government agent. I recalled how after settling into his new American life, Uncle Henik had opened a little butcher and grocery shop in a downtrodden section of Paterson, New Jersey. One afternoon, a group of teenagers ducked in and stole some canned goods. Uncle Henik lunged for his meat cleaver and chased them down the block. They had never seen the likes of this man. They tossed the cans back at him and his cleaver, and the word soon went through the neighborhood: "Don't mess with that Henik, He's crazy!"

He wasn't crazy, but when you've survived Auschwitz for three years, you're not going to cower before a few thugs in Paterson. If the Court did rule in a way that placed my uncle in jeopardy, including his deportation, I believe he would either fight or flee and find some way to survive, and I would never bet against him.

It wasn't just my uncle I was thinking about. It was also my parents. If Civiletti's argument prevailed, then those like my parents who had misstated their backgrounds upon entry to the United States could be treated no differently than war criminals. For my parents, the unknown wasn't just the High Court's impending decision. The unknown was also my parents' own history. If they were ever questioned about how they came to America—the circumstances of their subterfuge and their life with a false identity—what would they say? I had no idea.

Back at my building, I ran up the flight of stairs to my office, past the smells from Kentucky Fried Chicken below, to grab for the phone on my desk. I dialed my travel agent and within minutes had a flight booked to Miami. I then called my parents to tell them I was coming this weekend. I didn't want to alarm them, so I simply said an opportunity to see them had come up and I needed a break from Washington.

For the remainder of the week, I worked diligently while avoiding chats with my colleagues, determined to stay clear of anything that might expose my unease. The difference of philosophies, of means and objectives between me and my colleagues, was widening by the day.

My Diamond taxi, with its duo-toned banner of emerald and black emblazoned on its side, arrived promptly on Saturday morning. I kissed Joan and Daniela a rushed farewell, promising I'd be back soon.

The sun was just budging its way through the mid-autumn early-morning fog. I got in the cab, sat back, and let the life of the capital city rush by as the cab made its way down Rock Creek Parkway, a ribbon of federal property that wove its way past the adjacent litter-strewn streets to my left and then the tony townhouses and manicured sidewalks of Georgetown to my right. We headed across the Memorial Bridge toward Arlington National Cemetery and then swerved onto the George Washington Parkway to Washington National Airport, the dull glow of the Potomac River to my left.

Once in Miami, I rented a car and retraced the now-familiar route down Biscayne Boulevard to my parents' condo. I pressed the doorbell and Ma answered, an apron draped over her hips. For a second she seemed a bit hesitant, as if troubled by my arrival. But whatever gave her pause quickly dissolved into a warm embrace.

"*Ellenu!*" she gasped.

Dad appeared in the entryway. A thin cloud of concern seemed to hang over him but that too faded as he extended his hand to me, his eyes, as always, averting my direct gaze.

In no time we were back in the living room, taking my place on the white sofa with tropical flourishes that had been recently purchased to spruce things up. My parents sat in the old dark armchairs from the Bronx, and between us was the large mahogany cocktail table with its deep drawer bursting with photos from their past.

Ma set steaming cups of tea before us. She looked tan and much more fit than I had ever recalled. Florida seemed to agree with them both.

"So, Allan," Dad began, his tone warm but with a note of anxiety. "To what do we owe the pleasure of your visit?"

"I need to know something," I said, my eyes searching out his. "How did you manage, all those years, to carry the Blumstein name? And why was it necessary?"

His gaze dropped to the table and then lifted toward my mother.

"Ellenu," she sighed, her eyes locked on my father. "We had a bad feeling about your new job. Is that what this is about? Did something happen? I know you said something about an important Supreme Court argument. Is that what this is about? Tell me."

A moment of silence stretched on. Then Dad spoke before I could answer. "So, as you know, we adopted the Blumstein family name and their identity so we could come to America when the quota kept us out. They had gotten the visa; we didn't qualify. Does the Supreme Court hearing, if that is what this about, have something to do with that?"

I knew from my encounter with Saul Kies in Jerusalem that they had been allowed to revert to their Gerson surname, without penalty of deportation, because—or at least, so it was argued—they feared political persecution if they were ever forced return to Poland. But I had never thought much about it and had never even told them of my meeting with Kies. Strange, perhaps in retrospect, but at the time I simply wanted to get on with my life, and this seemed like a detail from long ago, or a detail I didn't care to know much about. There had been a name change, and that was that. I never dwelled on why my father couldn't bring himself to inform me but had to delegate that to his lawyer. But it happened, it worked, and life went on.

"Dad," I said, trying to appear levelheaded and not provoke any undue concern. "I think there may be more to the family narrative that was never discussed. Now, I need to understand it better. Tell me the whole story." My voice was soft but determined.

"We were afraid, Allan, that this might happen when you took your new job," Dad said. "Our worst fear was that our past could be used against you—that it would come up in the course of a background screening. Has that happened?"

"No, Dad," I answered quickly. "It's just that I've spent weeks wading through cases revolving around murky immigration law which may be fast changing, and for my own peace of mind, I need to know. I need to hear it from you."

My parents exchanged a nervous glance. We had all but forgotten our steaming glasses of black tea.

Dad turned to his small study off the bedroom. "I will be right back," he said. He returned with a turquoise folder with old yellow papers.

"Back in the DP camp in Austria," he started.

"Austria?" I interrupted. "I thought it was Germany."

"First, Austria, after Legnica."

"Legnica?"

"Yes, Legnica," he said as he turned to a faded piece of paper marked Foehrenwald, on which he had sketched out their travels. "After we had decided to go back to Zamość, with you in hand, about a year old, we started the long journey from Uzbekistan. Then as we neared Zamość, we heard about the Kielce pogrom. Your mother said never more, we are never going back to Zamość, there is nothing there for us, just tears for the death of all we left behind. And we are not welcome back. I know there is someone else, some other family, living in our home. But I don't care. I won't fight them, I haven't the strength. Let's turn around. Let's take the next train out of Poland."

"But of course, leaving Poland to go where, with a baby? Some people like us went to Palestine, but we knew it was like a war zone and that real war might come soon and your mother was not going there under these circumstances with you." She said she had suffered enough, and she was right."

We thought maybe we could make it to America. But had no family there, no sponsor, except a distant cousin in Long Island. But we had heard from others about the '*goldene medina,*' the golden land. But first we had to get into the American zone. The Russians were occupying Poland and weren't allowing immigration to America. Legnica was a town in the far corner of southwestern Poland that had been part of Germany, Silesia, until being transferred to Poland after the end of the war. So we went to a part of Poland that was really like Germany, but in any event, it would be our gateway to perhaps make it across to the American zone of occupation in Germany. And from there we hoped to come to America. But—"

"But?"

"But it wasn't that easy. We could only get as far as Austria, to Linz, where we were put into a ... what they called a DP camp but was really a detention center. There, we were told that life was better in Germany, in a large DP camp known as Foehrenwald near the German city of Wolfratshausen. But we needed new papers. For some reason, it was hard to get there, hard to get into that camp.

And then we met a couple whose name was Blumstein. They said they had transit papers that allowed them to go to Foehrenwald. And they had put their names on the application rolls to get a US visa. But they decided instead to go to Palestine. They said we could have their papers, if we wanted them. Actually, we had to pay a little bit. But that is what it was like then. They had a son named Abram Blumstein born on July 31, 1944. You were of course born on June 19, 1945. But you were always big, eleven pounds at birth, so it seemed possible for us to pass you for Abram.

Ma would become Rachel Blumstein, two years younger. And I would become Moszec Blumstein, who was also born in 1908. Your mother said, 'What do we have to lose?' So we took their papers and kept them, changing them a bit when we arrived in Foehrenwald, as he was a carpenter, about which I knew nothing, to get a certificate from the IRO, the International Refugee Organization, that said I was qualified as *'Buchfuhrer,'* a bookkeeper, and your mother qualified as *'Schneidermejsterin,'* a master seamstress."

"This all happened in early 1948. It took us that long to get across from Austria into the American zone of Germany and into Foehrenwald, and your mother was pregnant then and Sam was born April 1948 just as the war with Israel and the Arabs was starting, so we certainly weren't going there.

And life was good in Foehrenwald. There were many organizations there, and I became the deputy director of the Joint Distribution Committee, which was helping to run the camp, and you went to a wonderful kindergarten and we lived good, but it was temporary. Fortunately, very fortunately, we got notice, I would say in the fall, of approval of our visa for America and that we could leave to go there in December. Of course, it was under the name of Blumstein. We could account for Sam easily as he was born in Foehrenwald, so he could keep his actual age. So that's the whole story, dear Allan: now you know it."

"It's not really the whole story, is it?"

"You mean it's the story of what happened afterward, of what it means to be a refugee, with false papers, after our coming to America."

"That's what I mean."

Now Ma continued. "You should know, Jews like us weren't being welcomed to America then, even by many American Jews who thought they were better than the 'greeners'—the new Jews, especially those from Eastern Europe. In 1948, there was a new law in America for taking in DPs, but it made it nearly impossible to get a visa unless you had a family sponsor and a waiting job. We didn't have a relative in the United States, except this distant relative who we didn't really know, and besides his name was Morris Gerson, not Blumstein, and we had heard that he had spent some time in prison, so we couldn't really mention him on our papers. And we had no work lined up for us. There were exceptions. If you were a farmer under the DP law, you were admissible, regardless of job opportunity. But the Ukrainians were the farmers, not the Jews. So, what were we to do?"

Ma took a deep breath, still unnerved by the memory of that not so distant past. Dad continued. "So we said to ourselves, we will be the Blumsteins from now on, act as if we're them in the visa interviews, like actors on a stage, become each of the Blumstein family members. But I never wanted us, if I could avoid it, to get US citizenship under anything but our real names. And I never wanted you to be a Bar Mitzvah but as a Gerson."

He paused, rummaged through some papers suddenly, and looked up. "Here, look!" Here, look, here's the retainer agreement I signed with the attorney, Saul Kies, to try to make it happen. I had to pay him $1,000. No easy sum for us at that time. But we saved every penny we made aside from having to send you to a yeshiva. And the lawyer, Kies, said that if I testified to the court that if I were to be deported, along with my family, back to Poland, which was now under Communist rule, I would face political persecution—even though, to tell the truth, I was a bit of a Communist in my early years."

Dad said that, according to Kies, he was taking a risk, because the court might not believe him and Ma, and then they would lose their citizenship and face deportation.

"We could remain as Blumsteins indefinitely," he said, "or at least until caught. But I didn't want that. So I took the risk. I didn't want to hide any longer and always feel afraid of being discovered. And I wanted my children to have the family name—Gerson. Yet I knew it wouldn't be so easy for you, especially in the beginning. But we tried. And after another year at yeshiva where you had to do the explaining, we shifted schools from the yeshiva and sent you to regular high school. I don't think … I hope … you had no big problems in changing your name and age."

I sat back and let this all seep in. So strange. I felt no anger. Certainly not for my parents. I had grown up knowing so little about my parents' journey to the United States or of their travails in Siberia or Uzbekistan or the DP camps in Austria and then in Germany, let alone how they had to disguise themselves as someone else, dreaming of nothing more than to build a decent life for themselves, and especially their children. Now as I listened to my father's recitation and looked at that scrap of paper from 1950 in which he had sketched their long journey, a new appreciation dawned of what they had suffered, of worlds destroyed and worlds rebuilt, and the courage required to do what they did.

I could not entertain those thoughts for long, however. Of immediate concern was the Supreme Court hearing and how that decision might affect my parents.

If the Court were to accept the Government's argument, what would their defense be to a zealous prosecutor? Times change, and so do prosecutors with new administrations that may have no loyalty to the immigration policies, or declared exercises of discretion, of their predecessors. If my parents were interrogated, would they have to say that their desperation to come to the United States led them to misrepresent themselves to get into Foehrenwald, which was controlled by the US military, and ultimately to forge their true identities on their US visa applications? How the Supreme Court would decide *Fedorenko* could cast troubling light on my parents' deception. A new law-and-order government campaign aimed beyond nabbing Nazi collaborators might be turned on them. Ordinary rights and protections simply didn't apply to those charged with being illegal immigrants.

"So, I understand why you came in under their identity," I said, my voice strained. "But why didn't you correct the record earlier?"

"My son, I thought many, many times about correcting what we had done. It was terrible to live under someone else's name, living in the shadows, always afraid of being discovered," he said.

"Dad," I said, my voice practically a whisper. "I know it wasn't easy. I remember the hot dog incident."

"The ... hot dog incident?" He looked up toward my mother, confused.

"You remember, when we were coming out of Klein's?"

I recounted the incident for him, with the vendor calling out his real name and my dad's frightened reaction, and I wondered how many other vendors they encountered during those years, calling out "Gerson!" as my parents panicked.

Dad exhaled slowly. "Yes, yes I remember. We wanted to shield you, but it wasn't easy living hidden here, not after all we endured." not after all we had endured." He stood up and pulled open one of the credenza's doors, shuffling silently through a stack of binders. He withdrew one and pulled from it a sheet of paper.

"Let me show you something," he said, taking a seat on the sofa as he handed me a social welfare case file dated 1951. I could see that an unnamed social worker assigned to new arrivals from the Jewish Social Services Association had kept meticulous notes of each encounter with my parents. The social worker took issue with the fact that my father, still known as Blumstein, had been evasive with regard to his family in the States. Citing this fact, she refused to sign off on medical allowances that would allow my father to hold down a steady job while getting treatment for himself and my baby brother, who was ill at the time.

"When the welfare people began to suspect something was off with our identity documents, instead of offering any sort of guidance, they used the information to make life difficult for us," my dad said. "I won't say blackmail us, but they made me forego the medical allowances we had qualified for unless I reported to them that I had a relative here—the wealthy Morris Gerson from Long Island. But I wouldn't do it. We risked our last penny trying to protect ourselves from them, the very people who were supposed to be helping people like us."

"I realize you would have faced an uphill battle fighting this in court because of our identities," I said, "but why didn't you turn to friends or neighbors or other members of our community for help?"

"You might say," Ma responded slowly, choosing her words carefully, "as I said before, the American Jews didn't like us all that much. Sure, they did what they felt they had to do to help us, and we were grateful of course. But you know, they were a little ashamed of us Holocaust Jews. They would tell death camp survivors to roll down their sleeves, even on the hottest days of summer—they didn't want to see their concentration camp tattoos. 'We're not *showy* in this country,' they would say." Ma shook her head.

The longer I sat here, and the more they opened up and I listened, the less I seemed to know about my own childhood, as well as the struggles behind the scenes. I thought back to my youth spent studying at an ultra-Orthodox yeshiva. "Why didn't you send me to a normal public school if you had such disregard for the American Jews?" I asked.

Dad chimed in. "Your mother wanted you off the streets. We lived in a rough neighborhood in Brooklyn. And anyway, we figured it wouldn't hurt for you to have a little more Jewish culture in you than you would have gotten at a public school. Maybe we weren't so religious ourselves." He closed his eyes for a moment, as though trying to shake haunting memory from consciousness.

"Feh!" My mother intervened. "How could they believe in God after what happened? They said their prayers as if nothing had happened, as if God was still guiding his beloved people out of Egypt. Some 'beloved.'"

I had another question. "We were so firmly established as Blumsteins—why did you feel compelled to reclaim our original names?"

"Because they were our real identities," Ma answered sharply.

Then, softening her tone, she continued, "But why are you asking all this now? Can the government now take away our US citizenship?"

"No, Ma," I said, surprising myself with the assuredness of my tone. "Of course not. I just wanted to understand it all."

"Ellenu," Ma's voice cracked. "I was afraid that only bad would come out of this new job of yours. Now what should we do? What about Henik?"

I tried to remain composed for my parents' sake and not to betray my own concerns. "No one at OSI is going after Jewish survivors, Ma," I said, as if the very thought of it was unthinkable. Neither of my parents looked reassured.

There was nothing more I could say to assuage their concerns, or mine. But I did have one other question.

"So why, Dad, when it was all over, why didn't you tell me? Why did you leave it to the lawyer to tell me that I was a year younger and now had a different name?"

"I couldn't. That's all I can say," he said, his eyes fixed somewhere beyond my left shoulder. And the fact that he "couldn't" stuck with me. He could do all sorts of things. He could take all sorts of risks. But he couldn't tell me of this change because it would hurt him too much to see my bafflement. Strangely, his response only drew me closer to him.

In the years since, I've come to realize how resourceful my father had to have been to engineer such a scheme. It was that resourcefulness that helped him and his family survive all those years as refugees. But how do you make an entire family disappear—our family—and revive it as a different family with a different name? How do you do that without drawing the suspicion of military authorities, customs agents, immigration officials, social workers, employers, and civil bureaucrats? Was it just a coincidence that at Foehrenwald, my father became the deputy of the camp's Joint Distribution Committee, with access to its administrative paperwork, around the same time he secured family visas under the Blumstein name?

My parents kept copious records, but I can't find anything that explains how my father did what he did. He was a studious bookkeeper, and he surely used those skills in covering his tracks to ensure the safety of his family.

It pains me that my parents could never share their subterfuge with me, not until I was an adult and asked them myself. I understand why. They wanted to protect me. The less I knew about this history, the better, so I would not have to relive their pain: of deception, of fear, of material misrepresentation, of abandoning a treasured family name that dated back centuries so that the "remnant" of this generation might survive. Each day that they lived under an assumed identity was another day that they lived under a long shadow of memory and remorse. Once our name was restored, there was no reason to remind me, in my new identity, of what was lost and what was gained.

Allan holds his father's hand at a Displaced Persons camp march, ca. 1950.

Chapter Sixteen

Fedorenko's Verdict

I returned from Miami to OSI in a personal holding pattern, like a plane circling a runway waiting for clearance from ground control. Here ground control was the US Supremes and how they would rule on *Fedorenko,* and to a lesser extent, how the US District Court in Philadelphia would pronounce on the fate of Osidach. Their destinies and mine—and far more individuals than OSI ever intended to be affected—were now intertwined.

On January 21, 1981, a warmer-than-usual wintry day when snow had turned to slush, the US Supreme Court was, at noon, to hand down its ruling in *Fedorenko*. One could feel the tension mount as OSI awaited the culmination of this long litigation, begun before the unit was established but hovering ever since over all the work it did.

I set my briefcase in my office and headed for the break room. As I began pouring myself a cup of coffee, I heard Allan Ryan, who had taken over as Director of OSI in January, 1980, talking to other members of the staff about the imminent decision. It was clear that for him this promised to be a crowning moment. The long nights of research, the honed arguments before the Court, the balancing of individual responsibility—accountability—against the mitigating circumstances of time and place and the defense of coercion were all coming to a head as the Supreme Court Justices, in their own mysterious calculations, weighed competing arguments. Only they knew the outcome: whether their ruling would enlarge the reach of US immigration laws in denaturalization and deportation proceedings, or whether the ruling would chastise the Court of Appeals for having strayed beyond the confines of Nazis and Jews. Ryan toasted to a successful outcome, one that meant different things to the two of us.

As the minutes ticked by, I kept myself busy organizing my desk, filing away documents. In my mind it was already clear that my days at OSI were numbered. The idea that the Supreme Court could put in motion Fedorenko's deportation back to the Soviet Union, to the ultimate fate that it had in store for Nazi collaborators—with the issue of willing or unwilling assistance not even an afterthought—seemed wrong, unjust, and inconsistent with American values if not its national interests.

If the Supreme Court ruled in favor of the government, Federenko's return to the Soviets would constitute the death penalty, yet it came with none of the safeguards of a criminal trial. The proceedings against Fedorenko went beyond Nuremberg and the jurisprudence of war crimes tribunals. Here there had been no conviction, not even an indictment, no determination of an underlying crime.

Interesting, I mused, that neither the ACLU nor any other such organization had intervened in the name of civil liberties. To be sure, looking out for the rights of an alleged Nazi collaborator might not sit well with donors, but that's what civil liberties are about: defending the least popular or most offensive members in society, and we do that to ensure that everyone's liberties are defended.

A secretary interrupted my thoughts to hand me a copy of the judgment that had just come down.

I lunged for it right away, fumbling a "thank you." I could tell that the case had deeply divided the Justices. The heading read: Judgment of the Court of Appeals Affirmed, but the head note indicated dissents and concurrences. This would be complicated. I skimmed through the ruling of the majority—searching for the part that would deal with its interpretation of the 1948 DP Act that centered on "assistance" in persecution. I looked and looked but couldn't find it. Could it be that the majority opinion didn't touch on this critical issue, the mainstay of the government's argument that even involuntary assistance calls for revocation of citizenship and deportation?

I stopped skimming and began treading carefully through the majority opinion, and there I discovered the kernel of its reasoning: an interpretation of the law of its own making beyond what either the government or the defense had argued. The Supreme Court majority decided that the key issue in this case was not whether

Fedorenko had engaged in "assistance in persecution," but whether he had engaged in "persecution."

The majority opinion—signed by Justices Marshall, Brennan, Stewart, Powell, and Rehnquist—thus ruled in its key provision: "The solution to the problem [of jeopardizing the citizenship of Jewish survivors of extermination camps] ... lies, not in 'interpreting' the Act to include a voluntariness requirement that the statute itself does not impose, but in focusing on whether particular conduct can be considered assisting in the persecution of civilians. Thus, an individual who did no more than cut the hair of female inmates before they were executed cannot be found to have assisted in the persecution of civilians. On the other hand, there can be no question that a guard who was issued a uniform and armed with a rifle and pistol, who was paid a stipend and regularly allowed to leave the concentration camp to visit a nearby village, and who admitted to shooting at escaping inmates on orders from the commandant of the camp, fits within the statutory language about persons who assisted in the persecution of civilians. Other cases may present more difficult line-drawing problems, but we need decide only this case."

The majority in effect ruled that Ukrainian concentration camp guards *inherently* engaged in "persecution." Why the difference in focus? Hard to say. But with the focus on "persecution," the Court could more easily rule that concentration camp guard duty was inherently "persecution," because it said so; while cutting the hair of inmates or playing in the orchestra to confuse arrivals did not constitute "persecution," because, likewise, it said so. Reasoning in this fashion (tantamount to non-reasoning), the majority affirmed the revocation order of the courts below, clearing the way for Fedorenko's deportation.

Fancy footwork, I thought. Okay, Debby is clean. About Uncle Henik—not that I really knew what he had done, only that a stint as a *kapo* seemed possible—that was left open. Try as I might, the majority's logic in focusing on the word "persecution" rather than "assistance" eluded me: the issue of voluntariness was germane to both, but the majority sidestepped the question.

The ruling left prosecutors with little guidance. Only this was clear, to the extent there was any clarity: voluntariness was no longer the catchword. Now the standard was "persecution," whose meaning would be decided on a case-by-case basis, which would cause even more potential confusion.

Two other Justices—Chief Justice Burger and Justice Blackmun—sided with their brethren in the majority, though weakly: they said that the reasoning of the majority was not their own, nor one they could endorse, even though they came down on the same side.

Of the two concurring Justices, Blackmun seemed the more troubled. He expressed concern about the breadth of the ruling, fearing that it might open the door for revocation of US citizenship on the thin reed that full disclosure *might* have led to an investigation, which *might* have led to denial of a visa application. Nevertheless, despite pointing to the dangers in the majority's ruling, he added his name in concurrence.

Justices Stevens and White offered withering dissents, finding the majority's decision morally repugnant. Justice White, appalled by the lack of clarity in the ruling, dissented on the grounds that the case should be sent back to the Court of Appeals to specify the appropriate legal standard. That, he reasoned, was far preferable to the presumptuousness of the Supreme Court in fashioning an interpretation of the law on the basis of something of its own invention, one that had never been argued by either side in the courts below, thus only further muddling the issue.

Justice Stevens was even more vehement in his condemnation of the ruling.

"The majority has decided the case on a theory that no litigant argued, that the government expressly disavowed, and that may jeopardize the citizenship of countless survivors of Nazi concentration camps…The Court would give the word 'persecution' some not-yet-defined specially limited reading. In my opinion, the term 'persecution' clearly applies to such conduct [as cutting hair, etc.]; indeed, it probably encompasses almost every aspect of life or death in a concentration camp."

Justice Stevens argued that his colleagues were reacting to the horrors of Treblinka rather than adhering to the law: "The gruesome facts recited in this record create what Justice Holmes described as a sort of 'hydraulic pressure' that tends to distort our judgment."

My colleagues celebrated the Supreme Court ruling, touting it as a great victory for OSI and for Attorney General Civiletti. I sat alone in my office and began putting my thoughts about the decision into writing, which eventually found their way into a piece, "Beyond

Nuremberg," published in *Commentary* magazine on October, 1981. I was deeply ambivalent about the ruling. If "persecution" is the standard for culpability in a death camp, there is no doubt that Fedorenko was guilty: an armed guard's very function is to ensure that massive extermination proceeds without a hitch. But what of the Jews? As I wrote for *Commentary*, "It is painful even to contemplate asking those who survived, in circumstances where all conventions of normal life disappeared, whether survival was worth the price some had to pay. It is awful that this awful question should have been raised in the trial of one who was on the side of the murderers rather than of the murdered."

I reluctantly concluded that the Court's majority had come to the right decision: Had Justice Steven's view prevailed, the case would have been dismissed on the grounds that the government had failed to show that Fedorenko's actions were voluntary, and that would have meant condoning savagery. Perhaps a distinction could have been drawn between the obligations of a soldier, which Fedorenko had been, and civilians, but the Court chose never to do so. Rather, I wrote, it "fashioned its own dialectic, roughly hewn, painful to swallow, but morally responsive to the difficult challenge posed by this troubling case." In time, however, I have come to be less sanguine about the Supreme Court's decision, believing that the Court should have hewed to the "voluntary" standard and remanded the case. The District Court would then have been compelled to determine whether, as a matter of fact, Federenko had acted willingly or, alternatively, under the pain of coercion that deprived him of free will.

There was nothing ambivalent about Fedorenko's fate. Stripped of his US citizenship, he was ordered deported in 1983. He chose the Soviet Union, which had previously assured him that he faced no criminal liability. But the Soviets had recently tried and executed a naturalized Belgian citizen accused of war crimes, and Fedorenko gave them the same opportunity to send a message about what happens to anyone who betrayed the homeland. Fedorenko was deported in 1984, and the Soviets tried him for desertion, taking punitive actions against civilians, and participating in mass executions. He was found guilty and sentenced to death. This should have come as no surprise to anyone involved in the prosecution or adjudication of this case. He was 78 years old when the bullets ripped through his frame.

From 1981-1986 Allan Gerson served as counsel to the U.S. Delegation to the United Nations.

Chapter Seventeen

Till the Ends of Justice

By the time the Osidach ruling came down several weeks later, I'd prepared my letter of resignation but had yet to submit it. I was still holding out hope that the court would find a way to achieve what the survivors wanted: holding the collaborators accountable without overreaching into the realm of unbridled prosecutorial discretion.

Once the hard copy of the ruling reached our office, I started tearing through its pages. I felt calmer the moment I saw that Judge Bechtle had begun his ruling with a concise history of Ukrainian involvement in Nazi-ordered massacres. That augured well, for it was precisely the historical context that I had hoped might form part of the judgment. In this way, the judicial opinion might transform itself from a mere routine application of law and into a broader exploration of why this case was important enough to have been brought so many years after the facts. I hoped its findings and conclusion would go beyond legal jargon and tortured statutory construction to clarify why accountability, properly handled, mattered not only for those directly affected, the persecuted, but for all of Americans concerned with coming to grips with a horrendous past, especially when its chief perpetrators were in our midst, leading perhaps productive, but certainly undisturbed lives.

It is hard to know what goes on in a judge's mind as he crafts his ruling. But on reading Judge Bechtle's opinion, it became immediately apparent that the testimony of our expert witness, Raul Hilberg, had left its mark. Judge Bechtle concluded that while Hilberg's testimony did not constitute proof, in eye-witness or documentary form, of the collaboration of the Ukrainian police in the murder of Rawa-Ruska's Jews, it nevertheless "serves to show that what occurred in that town was not an isolated instance of conduct but totally consistent with a general pattern of persecutorial conduct throughout the Galicia region." As to Osidach's counter argument that the Ukrainian police were never involved in the *particular* case of the liquidation of the Jews of Rawa-Ruska, Judge Bechtle ruled that the assertion, as a matter of historical record, was "not credible, or believable ... In simplest terms, Osidach's version is completely at odds with the realities of life in Rawa-Ruska during the German occupation ... [as] without doubt Osidach was a voluntary and willing member of the Ukrainian police in 1942-1944." Accordingly, Osidach was rightfully declared, however many years after the fact, "ineligible to enter this country in 1949 as a displaced person."

What more could I have asked for? Here was a complete and lengthy judicial record of Ukrainian police collaboration in the slaughter of the Jews of Rawa-Ruska, symptomatic of what they had done throughout Nazi-occupied Ukraine. Moreover, Osidach was found to have been a "voluntary and willing" participant in genocide, no mere captured soldier forced, as Federenko claimed, to survive on grass when half his compatriots had already succumbed to death by starvation, or save himself by donning the uniform of a concentration camp guard with carbine in hand.

But then Judge Bechtle's opinion veered off into strange territory, much as the US Supreme Court had done in its handling of *Fedorenko*. Instead of ruling that Osidach, on the basis of these facts, had not been eligible for a US entry visa in 1949 under the Displaced Persons Act's prohibition of entry to those who "have assisted the enemy in persecuting civil populations," he entered a ruling based on a theory that the government had never advanced.

Judge Bechtle focused on a section of the DP Act that disqualifies entry of displaced persons by individuals who had any affiliation with "movements" that had been involved in assisting the enemy in the persecution of civilians during the Second World War, and that the OUN during the war had been one such "movement." Judge Bechtle's interest in "movements" was never fully explained, though perhaps he thought it more in line with the Supreme Court's focus on "persecution." In any event, he declared that mere membership in a movement dedicated to persecuting civilians is sufficient to strip one of US citizenship, regardless of any personal participation in persecution. In later years, the State Department would maintain a list of designated terrorist organizations, and forwarding any money to such organizations can draw a penalty of up to 15 years in prison. The debate still rages whether the practice of mere membership in a designated terrorist organization, without proof of any terroristic activity outside of financial contributions, should be sufficient to warrant extreme penalties.

But why Judge Bechtle would want to introduce this idea in the Osidach case, where his actions had already been determined to be those of a willing participant, was unclear to all of us at OSI. He had already ruled that Osidach was, personally, a willing participant. A wider ruling about organizational membership seemed wholly unnecessary and could provide an opening for appeal on the grounds that it was Osidach himself, or at most the Ukrainian police force in Rawa-Ruska, but certainly not the OUN that was on trial with an opportunity to defend itself.

It seemed that Judge Bechtle anticipated such a challenge, for he went to great lengths to point out that while mere membership in a hostile organization could not be used to strip an American citizen of his rights, here we were dealing with aliens, and that when aliens apply for visas, they have no ordinary due process rights. Thus, in a ringing conclusion that revolved around the sovereign prerogatives of the United States to protect its borders in the name of national security interests, he wrote: "We are dealing here with the exercise of the Nation's sovereign power to admit or exclude foreigners in accordance with perceived national interests."

Again, I felt squeezed and disheartened. First in *Fedorenko* and now here, by twists and turns, rulings that should and could have easily centered on the crucial fact that defendants were willing executioners instead careened into unchartered territory beyond what had been argued. In the case of *Osidach*, the District Court chose to hold that as a matter of law, mere membership in a hostile organization is sufficient—without any proof of individual misconduct—to justify the revocation of US citizenship.

Was I being too hard on the judge? After all, we had won. The results were good.

A firm record had been established on how the Ukrainian police had collaborated with the Nazis in the destruction of the Jews. Despite past failures in ferreting out Nazi collaborators, we had now established a standard of justice, a moral compass, and

Osidach himself would be held accountable for what he had done to the Jews of Rawa-Ruska.

And yet … at what price victory? I yielded to no one in my determination to see to it that Osidach's role in enabling the Holocaust be exposed for all to see. And if the law provided for denaturalization and, in its wake, deportation as the appropriate remedy for those who had lied about their wartime complicity to gain entry into America, then by all means apply the law to the hilt.

Yet, where the law was vague, and being shaped as it was here by judges who heard these cases from the lowest courts to the highest, there was another voice that rang true for me. This was of the biblical lesson: "Justice, justice shall ye pursue," the pursuit of justice by just means. That is what Nuremberg was all about.

But US immigration law is a flimsy instrument, and the accused are presumed to have few rights, not least to a demonstration that they are responsible for their actions because they were the product of free will. On this ground alone, it seemed to me that Osidach and Federenko deserved the punishment that was meted out to them. But for whatever reason, this essential component was skirted by the courts and prosecutors alike, perhaps in the impetus to score as many "wins," as many deportations or successful denaturalizations, as possible.

Perhaps my being the child of illegal immigrants who had faced deportation had skewed my judgment; any law, ruling, or regulation that seemed arbitrary, or needlessly harsh against undocumented immigrants, simply because they were undocumented immigrants, made me suspicious. The Osidach ruling gnawed at me precisely because the net it cast was way too wide. The judgment was fraught with the danger of enabling a rush to revocation of US citizenship not only on the basis of the absence of the rights of due process that accrue in the most ordinary criminal trial, but now, by judicial fiat, by a show of mere membership in "movements."

Beyond the long reach of the ruling, there was the image of Osidach himself—a desiccated old man, wheezing, baffled, desperately sucking oxygen through the thin plastic lines connected to his portable oxygen tank. Was I to be ashamed for wondering whether the ends of justice—and OSI was formed for a particular type of "special" justice centered on the enablers of Nazi atrocities living in America—would be served by deporting Osidach, now a shadow of his former self to the Soviet Union, the only country that wanted him, and where he would undoubtedly face summary execution? I told myself I had nothing to be ashamed of in harboring such thoughts, no more than the Israeli witness who stood next to Osidach at the urinal and held the door for him as they both exited, for revenge had turned stale and all he wanted and now dreamed of was a record for his children and his grandchildren and to let those witnesses carry forth the truth.

As the son of Holocaust survivors, I had every reason to scream for retribution, to put aside any thoughts of mercy based on age or infirmity. But as I watched the proceedings unfold, I could not escape thinking that I was also the product of a religious tradition— orthodox Judaism— that calls for tempering justice with mercy. At my Yeshiva, I learned early on with rapt attention the Biblical story of God preparing to destroy the evil city of Sodom, and that Abraham intervened to ask God these questions:

Abraham prefaces the exchange by asking God: "Shall not the Judge of all the World do Justice?"

"What if there are 50 righteous people in Sodom? Would you still destroy it?"

God says no, he would spare Sodom for 50 righteous people.

Abraham asks, "what if there are 45 righteous people?"

God offers the same answer, that He would spare the city for 45 righteous people.

And the negotiation unfolds, with God assuring Abraham that He will not sweep away Sodom even if it has only 10 righteous people. But that's the limit.

Abraham's plea for God to show mercy for the sake of the few righteous in evil's midst was for me the quintessential question: Is justice untempered by mercy still justice?

I also vividly recalled from my youth the sermon on the meaning of the passage in Deuteronomy (16:20): *"Justice, justice you shall pursue"* as an invocation to pursue justice by just means, to temper where one can the harsh unfeeling letter of the law with the oft-repeated appeal in daily prayer to *al-Rahum v' Chanum*: (translated the same in Arabic as in Hebrew) God of mercy and compassion.

Try as I might, I could see nothing useful to be gained by going beyond stripping Osidach of his US citizenship to deport him to the Soviet Union, or elsewhere. Not at this stage of his life, not in his condition. Of course, that never meant to me that OSI was misguided in its purpose. Congress had spoken, reflecting a new national mood: No longer would we sweep the awareness of the Nazi-enablers' deeds under the national rug. They had to be exposed, their US citizenship stripped, and a robust historical record created of what they had enabled. All this was to ensure that we never forget and, in many aspects, never forgive, but always mindful that we ourselves do harm, mindful that deportation is an awesome matter, a mighty tool that should never be wielded without attention to its consequences.

My reservations about the *Osidach* ruling became moot when he suffered his massive fatal heart attack, less than two months after the Court handed down its decision. Whether due to the stress of the trial and the ruling, or whether he had sped his demise by refraining from taking his six daily heart medications, no one will ever know. What is indisputable is that his life came to its end while both the United States and the Soviet Union, each for its own reasons, were eager to see him deported, and the US courts were clearly ready to find novel reasons to speed his departure.

My tenure at OSI had run its course. The pressures of the job were taking a heavy emotional toll. The thought that I could separate my professional responsibilities from my personal history proved illusory, and it filled me with internal contradictions. At times, I was ready to play the role of the angel of my parents' redemption; at other times I was repulsed by the idea, as if it were a youthful dream.

Always, at OSI as elsewhere, I felt I was the outlier. Winning never meant the same to me, it seemed, as it did to the others. Professional prosecutors often present the world as narrowly confined clashes between the oppressor and the victim, the sinner and the saint. But the world was never divided that easily for me. I shared with all those at OSI the goal of bringing Nazi collaborators to justice. But for me, the quest began where for many others it ended. I saw strict enforcement of US immigration laws, for these particular defendants, as a way-station to a larger purpose: understanding what motivated the collaborators, perhaps to deter a repeat of mass savagery and destruction, in any part of the world, for any reason, at any time.

We express our values as a nation because we must, and inevitably they revolve around key principles in the Declaration of

Independence; most notably, that all men are created with certain inalienable rights, upon which the framers pledged our "lives, our fortunes and our sacred honor." Those rights, however, are held by the grant of US citizenship. Strip a man or a woman of that citizenship, and those rights disappear. When that happens, deportation—among other judicial assaults—can be easily countenanced precisely because those individuals are no longer American citizens. That is why US citizenship should be the hardest right to lose, but it is not.

My parents had reason to be worried. We were, as my father said, getting them on lies, and "we all lied."

It was time to leave OSI. I did not begrudge or make light of its purpose, but I saw life through a different lens, and there was no looking glass through which I could adjust that lens to my own tastes and sensibility. I politely said my goodbyes. I wished them all well. Eighteen months had passed since I began the job, but I felt as if I had lived a lifetime, rediscovered my past, understood my parents better, met historic figures, and born witness to the great tragedy of our times. In the process, I was able to glimpse into the minds of some of those who had enabled man's most ignoble moment.

Whatever I learned, it was now my responsibility to remember, to bear witness, to preserve, and to share. For history has a tendency to repeat it itself in variations that elude our grasp, leaving no nationality or ethnic group immune from its scourge. And we will always look to the resources of the rule of law to provide a moral compass. Here, I would hope, my own experience with OSI, its pitfalls and high points, lays down markers of what might be hoped for, and what might be expected.

I am reminded of the lines in A. Sutzkever's poem:

"Who Will Remain? What Will Remain?"

Remembrance of three flamingos at Lake Victoria,
Revealed to me in their full splendor and glory.
... And what gnaws at me is the curious question:
Three stringed flamingoes, do they remember,
To whom they belong?
Once in a lifetime are you granted such an encounter:
To see, to hear, to long

Allan Gerson and his son, David, at the Zamosc Memorial site in Paramus, New Jersey, 1998.

Epilogue

Encountering History

Nearly 40 years have passed since my year and a half at OSI. The passage of time has hardly robbed that period of its meaning. On the contrary, the events of the day bring me back nearly every day to that period, to lessons learned, and their applicability to the exigencies of the moment. It hardly needs to be said that any linkage, albeit tenuous, is not without spurs to examination of the proper means by which to view undocumented immigrants, and of deportations as the remedy of choice.

Woven into this tapestry is the question of due process or its absence in denaturalization and deportation proceedings. My experiences force me to consider whether abuse of prosecutorial discretion is enabling overly zealous prosecutors to bring such proceedings where the passage of time or acculturation in America may have dulled their probity and moral value, when the defendants have become transformed into far different persons than the one they were decades ago.

The courts of today, not unlike OSI in its lesser moments, have so narrowed their focus as to ignore the punitive consequences of deportation. If in OSI's time, judges were oblivious to the fact that firing squads awaited those deported to Russia, today, as I learned when I recently argued a *pro bono* case on behalf of a person seeking political asylum rather than face deportation to Honduras, judges are oblivious to whether returning a defendant to, for example, Honduras, might mean a police-style execution.

On a personal level, questions that erupted during my time at OSI still cry out for answers. How, precisely, did my family survive Siberia? Why did they not embrace my decision to join OSI? How did Aunt Raya—no longer of the living—manage to preserve the bundles of photographs that she risked saving in the war to become my precious keepsakes of another era? How did Uncle Henik manage to survive three years at Auschwitz? And will I ever stop hearing the words of Ida, recalling her jumping from a moving train headed to Belzec? "The others said I was crazy, but no one tried to stop me."

For my parents, as for so many survivors, the creation of OSI meant that the US government really cared about their plight in its determination to undertake a clean sweep of the Nazi collaborators in America who came here in such great numbers alongside the Jewish remnant. Still, they harbored reservations. For they were not only Holocaust survivors; they also carried the burden of lives as immigrants, lived for so many years under forged aliases. That gave particular consciousness to the danger of unbridled prosecutorial zeal. For the hand focused on Nazi collaborators one day, might turn on them on another. And might not friends who outwardly rendered some measure of "assistance" to their Nazi tormentors themselves become the targets of inquiry?

I had my special reasons for concern. If OSI failed to demonstrate that the actions of those it would denaturalize or deport were voluntarily rendered, would that not gut OSI's mission of its moral underpinning? What purpose would be gained by punishing the unwilling or coerced?

Were those fears overblown?

Two cases—both after I left OSI—show that while OSI had occasion to fall prey to overly zealous prosecution, and perhaps abuse of prosecutorial discretion, the threat was short-lived, damaging OSI's reputation, but not ushering in the deluge that my parents feared. The first concerns the matter of Ivan the Terrible; the second, the matter of Jacob Tannenbaum, a Jewish *kapo*.

John Demjanjuk, aka Ivan the Terrible, was a Ukrainian conscript who was drafted into the Red Army, captured, and made a prisoner of war, and he served as a guard at several death camps in Poland. He entered the United States in 1952 and became a naturalized citizen in 1958. In the late 1970s, even before the creation of OSI, the federal government charged Demjanjuk with unlawfully entering the United States by concealing his service at the death camps, including Treblinka. OSI took over the case in 1981, and with information it obtained from the Soviet Union, it charged that

Demjanjuk was "Ivan the Terrible," a particularly sadistic guard at Treblinka who enjoyed mutilating prisoners on their way to the gas chambers.

I learned early on that OSI harbored misgivings about contradictory evidence pinning Ivan Demjanjuk of Cleveland, Ohio, to Ivan the Terrible. But there was near-certainty at OSI that if he did not serve as a guard at one concentration camp, he was a guard at another. With that in mind, potential evidentiary discrepancies took short shrift. A friend of mine with a senior position in Israel's Foreign Ministry asked if Israel should ask for Demjanjuk's extradition to stand trial, like Eichmann in 1962, on charges of crimes against the Jewish people and crimes against humanity. I hesitated to offer encouragement. Aside from questions about discrepancy in evidence, Israel would have a tough road to hoe in charging him with war crimes, as his conviction would rest on meeting a much higher standard of proof than that required in OSI "civil" proceedings.

As it turned out, in 1981 OSI succeeded in revoking Demjanjuk's US citizenship, and in 1986 he was extradited to Israel, which found that he was indeed Ivan the Terrible and sentenced him to death. But while his conviction was under appeal, the Soviet Union collapsed, and new evidence emerged that Demjanjuk was not in fact Ivan the Terrible and had not even worked at Treblinka, though he had worked at other death camps. The case wound its way up to the Israel Supreme Court, which had to concede that OSI had fingered the wrong person and that as there was no clear evidence to justify his further detention, he was set free. By this time, he had already spent nearly seven years in jail in Israel. In 1993, Demjanjuk returned to the United States to be with his family, and in 1998 the US Court of Appeals for the Sixth Circuit upheld the restoration of his US citizenship (pursuant to a claim filed by Demjanjuk and his lawyers) after lambasting OSI for having withheld exculpatory evidence.

In 1999, OSI persisted in filing a new denaturalization complaint against Demjanjuk for serving at other death camps—Sobibor and Majdanek in Poland, and Flossenburg in Germany. His US citizenship was again revoked, and he was deported to Germany, where in 2011, at age 91, he was convicted as an accessory in the murder of more than 28,000 Jews. He died before his appeal could be heard.

Only partial justice had been rendered. No final judgment had been secured against him despite 30 years of legal wrangling and his lengthy incarceration abroad. As for OSI, its very public and protracted misidentification of Ivan the Terrible exacted a heavy cost both on its resources and moral authority. Yet had it not been for Demjajnjuk's prosecution in a German court—the first against a non-German national for Nazi war crimes—a later deportation to Germany of a non-German national to stand trial for war crimes might not have been possible. In August 2018, Jakiw Palij, a Polish-born naturalized American citizen who had served as a Nazi concentration camp guard, dubbed by the *New York Times* as "the last Nazi in America," was deported to stand trial in Germany after having been stripped of his US citizenship. The matter is ongoing.

These prosecutions occurred after my time at OSI, but seeds had been planted while I was there. Each encompassed drawing a balance between fairness and due process and drawing a curtain on the accomplices to the Final Solution. There are no easy ways to the right balance. Each case and set of circumstances are unique. Each requires an independent negotiation between honoring civil liberties and rendering justice against the enablers—if not architects—of that great evil.

Beyond the balancing of civil liberties came another balancing act that I, and especially my parents, worried about. After OSI's early victories against Osidach and Fedorenko, Jewish Holocaust survivors like Debby seemed at risk. As a young musician she had lulled deportees to Auschwitz to their death by the sweet music emanating from the platform where the orchestra played. Could a prosecutor, unchecked in his zeal, not charge her with "assistance" to Nazi persecution?

A case in 1977 seemed to confirm those fears. Jacob Tannenbaum was a 77-year-old Brooklyn resident who had lost his father, wife, and five children in three concentration camps. He was also a Jewish *kapo* during the war who allegedly beat and possibly even killed Jewish prisoners, even though he had already lost most of one eye and could not stand straight because he had been beaten so often. Tannenbaum denied all charges against him.

When the denaturalization proceeding was announced, Walter Rockler, long-retired, railed against his successor at OSI, Neal Sher, for bringing the case, claiming that OSI's detractors could now draw a moral equivalence between the acts of Jewish *kapos* and the collaborators that OSI was supposed to be prosecuting. I shared that concern, even as I watched these proceedings from afar.

Tannenbaum, already frail, became ill during the court proceedings, and a settlement was reached: He agreed to be denaturalized on the grounds that he had brutalized prisoners, but the government agreed not to deport Tannenbaum until his health improved. It never did. He died in 1989, still in the United States.

OSI investigated other Jewish *kapos* but did not initiate any other proceedings against Jews who had worked in any capacity in the concentration camps, nor against Jews who had misled immigration authorities to enter the United States. Discretion prevailed. Common sense triumphed. My own fears—and those of my parents—did not come to pass. And yet I recognized, then as today, that abuse of prosecutorial discretion is amoeba-like, capable of transfiguring itself and reemerging in many different guises.

By the nature of its work, OSI was term-limited, as the passage of time continued to thin the ranks of perpetrators. In 2004, President George W. Bush signed into law the Intelligence Reform and Terrorism Prevention Act, which, among other things, enlarged OSI's function to include jurisdiction over anyone "who participated at any time outside the US in genocide…or extrajudicial killings." But in enlarging OSI's functions, the Holocaust, too, as the principal object of OSI's concern, was thinned out, relegated to now being but one of many genocides, albeit the most terrible in its destructive sweep, vying for OSI's attention.

The final death knell came in March 2010, when OSI, as an independent unit, officially came to an end. US Attorney General Eric Holder decided to merge OSI with the Domestic Security Section to create the Human Rights and Special Prosecutions Section (HRSP). Its mission, as described on the Justice Department website, makes no mention of rendering justice to those whose collaboration had enabled the Holocaust. Instead, focus is placed on the mission of HRSP to bring cases "against human rights violators and other international criminals…[including] violators for genocide, torture, war crimes, recruitment or use of child soldiers, female genital mutilation, international antiquities trafficking, and for immigration and naturalization fraud arising out of efforts to hide their involvement in such crimes." It had all become one big potpourri.

To be sure, OSI had won rulings against 108 participants in Nazi-sponsored persecutions, 68 of whom were deported or extradited. But while this figure is significantly higher than such prosecutions by any other country, one must bear in mind that the United States is alone among the world's nations engaged in such efforts in using a civil standard of proof, one (even if augmented by the "clear and convincing" standard employed in immigration proceedings) rather than the beyond-a-reasonable-doubt standards that usually apply to defendants in criminal trials. American judges did their best when confronted with OSI's cases, but consistent rulings were elusive. The judges were divided about whether free will really mattered in the maw of a death camp, and they were also uncertain about whether punishment must be tempered with mercy when defendants appeared as shadows of their former selves.

In the interim, US prosecutors have of late become emboldened in their zeal to deport children of undocumented aliens: "dreamers" who came to America many years ago under their parents' coattails. As I pointed out in a recent Op-Ed in the Washington Post, had my own immigrant status not been clarified in 1958 when my parents, and I derivatively, finally acquired US citizenship in our own names, I too, like the dreamers of today, would be subject to deportation. For unlike murder, robbery and battery, no statute of limitations exists for the perpetrators of immigration fraud.

OSI never operated in a vacuum. While I feared that the rulings in OSI cases might spill over into cases involving deportation of non-Nazi collaborators, the opposite was true. Non-OSI prosecutions were being pursued at a harsher pace than those by OSI. A ruling by the US Supreme Court on June 22, 2017, illustrates how federal prosecutors, operating on a parallel statute that OSI employed, one that metes out criminal penalties, sought to strip US citizenship for even the most petty and inconsequential of lies. It took the Supreme Court in the recent case of *Maslenjak vs. United States* (2017) to put an end to that effort. But the halt may prove temporary as the composition of the Supreme Court shifts and the three reluctant concurring opinions in that case seek exceptions in new cases.

The idea that the Justice Department would try to deem all lies equal still sends a shiver down my spine. For as has long been recognized, some facts are "material," and others are not. Exercising the authority vested in them, judges are there to separate the wheat from the chaff, the material from the immaterial. Not all lies are equal. Plato spoke of "truthful lies." If a lie about a minor traffic infraction that one was embarrassed to mention—which would, if disclosed, have no bearing on the grant of a visa—is nevertheless sufficient to strip one of US citizenship, then woe to us all. This indeed is my what my parents feared in the specter of unbridled prosecutorial discretion. Movement in that direction has been halted, but it will take eternal vigilance to ensure against its resurrection.

True, OSI never argued for opening as wide a net as the one the Justice Department urged in *Maslenjak*. But in successfully arguing in *Federenko* that any lie that *might* have led to an investigation that *might* have led to the non-grant of an entry visa was sufficient for revocation of US citizenship, it came perilously close.

After I left OSI, I spent (on the recommendation of my old mentor, Eugene V. Rostow, who expressed none of the diffidence he did when asked about my joining OSI) five years working as special counsel for the US ambassador to the United Nations, Jeane J. Kirkpatrick, and then another year for her successor, General Vernon A. Walters. My parents took pride that both ambassadors—they needed little prompting from me, but I helped give form to their instincts— repeatedly decried on the UN floor that whatever misgivings one might have about Israel's role in Middle East peace, resort to the term "Nazi-like" was not only ahistorical but abhorrent.

In 1986, I returned to the Justice Department as a DAAG (deputy assistant attorney general) in the Office of Legal Counsel and as counselor on international affairs. I then did a stint at a Washington think tank, taught law and policy at George Mason University, and worked at the Washington office of a Wall Street law firm.

My career then took a turn to protecting the victims of state-sponsored terrorism, first in the case of the Pan Am 103 terrorist bombing over Lockerbie, Scotland, in 1988, attributed to Libya, and then on behalf of families of victims of the 9/11 World Trade Center bombing linked to Saudi operatives. The former case was settled for a significant sum; the latter is still ongoing.

These engagements feature a common thread with the experience of my parents and other Holocaust survivors. I have sought to help people not to go through life doubly victimized, first by the atrocity, and then by a grinding sense of impotence at being unable to do anything about it. I have tried to be their voice in ending that frustration and achieving some measure of justice.

As for my parents, I must say that they were glad when my time at OSI came to an end. It was well and good to proclaim "never forget" and "never forgive" as their eternal mission, but in fact I doubted that they wanted me for any length of time to be left staring into the abyss that almost consumed them or confronting, face-to-face, the tormentors of their people.

My father had some good years left in Florida, where he headed up an active Yiddish cultural club, and he spent his final years in Washington, where in addition to teaching classes on Yiddish language and culture, he acted out plays for my children. Even while preoccupied by cancer operations and other medical issues, he still had time to develop a close friendship with Herman Taube, an outstanding Yiddish poet who was a medic with the Russian forces that liberated Auschwitz.

When my father was nearly on his deathbed, a last effort at surgery was attempted, and a dutiful surgeon, asking him routine questions, inquired of the cause of his parents' death.

"Gas," my father replied.

The puzzled surgeon asked him to explain himself.

"Gas chamber," my father said. "They died of gas chamber."

My brother Sam and I who witnessed the exchange later asked him why he'd been so aggressive in his answers.

"So that he should know who he is operating on," he said.

He died in 1991 and is buried at the Zamość Memorial site in New Jersey, his gravestone inscribed: *"Ohev Yiddish,"* a lover of Yiddish. In my eulogy, I wrote: "He wasn't always easy to understand. At times his world was impenetrable. But it continues to open up more and more." Indeed, the writing of this book has enabled me for the first time to appreciate the depth of his ordeal as a Holocaust survivor who had to carry the additional burden of being deemed an illegal immigrant with false documentation, living with his wife and children under names other than his own. I became in a way the reader of his tears, the interpreter (though far from complete) of his deceptions, and finally the inheritor of his love. For beyond honoring memory and the fallen, beyond all he had endured, was his acute power to persevere and never let go, finding dignity and revival in the beauty of language and poetry.

My mother lived on, and she conveyed her love and sensibility, shaped by a unique eye for the beautiful, so that she could be awed by the color white, to her grandchildren in multiple ways, sewing their costumes and bestowing coloring books filled with her sketches and drawings. Like my father, however, she remained haunted by the past, only more so: she would nightly hear the echoes of her sister pleading not to be left behind in Zamość and her father warning not to travel with her baby. She died in 1998. At her memorial service, in deference to her lifelong questioning of how an all merciful God could exist, instead of the usual religious litany we sang The Partisans Song: "Never say you are going down that last road."

My parents left an indelible mark on my children, as they absorbed in various but telling degrees a sense of responsibility as second-generation survivors.

I took my older daughter, Daniela, to Zamość in her junior year of college. As we began to cross the tracks to the area where we were told many gravestones abounded, we were taken aback by the scream of a train whistle as the cars roared past us to a destination marked "Belzec." Belzec is infamous for its gas chambers, but it's a town as well, and the end point of daily locomotives. Still, we trembled as that train sped by, as if caught in some terrible time warp, as if a reminder that absent luck and savvy, my own parents would have been on a train to Belzec, and my daughter and I would not be standing there that day.

As we crossed the tracks, we noticed a stout, bedraggled man sitting on a bench and staring ahead at the gravestones. We introduced ourselves and asked about those stones. We saw the markers signifying that the buried had died at Auschwitz. Only two bore the Star of David; the others bore crosses. The man explained that after the Jews of Zamość were eradicated, the non-Jewish Poles followed, all ethnically cleansed from the town to make room for the envisioned Himmlertown, where Zamość would be resettled by ethnic Germans.

Zamość today is a picturesque town with houses painted in pastel colors, a delight for tourists who want to experience an ideal city from the 16th Century Renaissance. Its nearby Bug River is today a destination spot for rafters and whitewater enthusiasts (the peaceful and shallow waters at its mouth giving rise 15 kilometers north to more difficult challenges). And if these rafters are assiduous enough to look at the surrounding terrain, they might notice the remains of train trestles adopted by the Wehrmacht with more extended gauge tracks for the trains bound west across the Bug River to Belzec, Sobibor, and Treblinka.

Daniela now works as an assistant professor of journalism at California State University, Northridge and heads up an immigration news project that covers the enormous number of migrants fleeing from Latin America and the Middle East. Her wife, Talia, is an accomplished immigration lawyer in Los Angeles who specializes in assisting undocumented immigrants, often seeking political asylum for them when they are faced with deportation. Talia's family on her father's side is also from Zamość.

My younger daughter, Merissa, when she was a junior in high school, spent a lot of time with my mother, seeking to comfort her when horrible memories induced panic attacks. Today Merissa writes and speaks often on intergenerational trauma.

My son David, who graduated in 2016 from the American Film Institute in Los Angeles, won a student Oscar for the short film called "All These Voices." The plot revolves around post-Holocaust theatrical performers coming to grips with their recent past in a dusty old theater where a young SS soldier has taken refuge. The following summer, David spent most of his time doing a documentary film on the refugees streaming into the Greek city of Lesbos.

By some twist of fate, my parents' deportation to Siberia enabled them to cheat death and ultimately allowed me to witness their rebirth in America. As destiny would have it, my work at OSI allowed me to encounter history, and those efforts enabled me to transform my parents' mysteries and suffering into the balm of justice. That is what OSI at its best represented for those who had stared into the abyss.

My father passed down to me the 1,200-page memorial book *Annals of Zamość*. When I open it, I behold photographs and reflections of a world that once glowed in the special light of a highly unusual town, cultured and attuned to beauty, which gave life and learning to so many. I recently had the book rebound and cleaned so that its embossed gold and red letters, emblematic of the flames that would engulf that way of life, shine on.

Photo Gallery

203

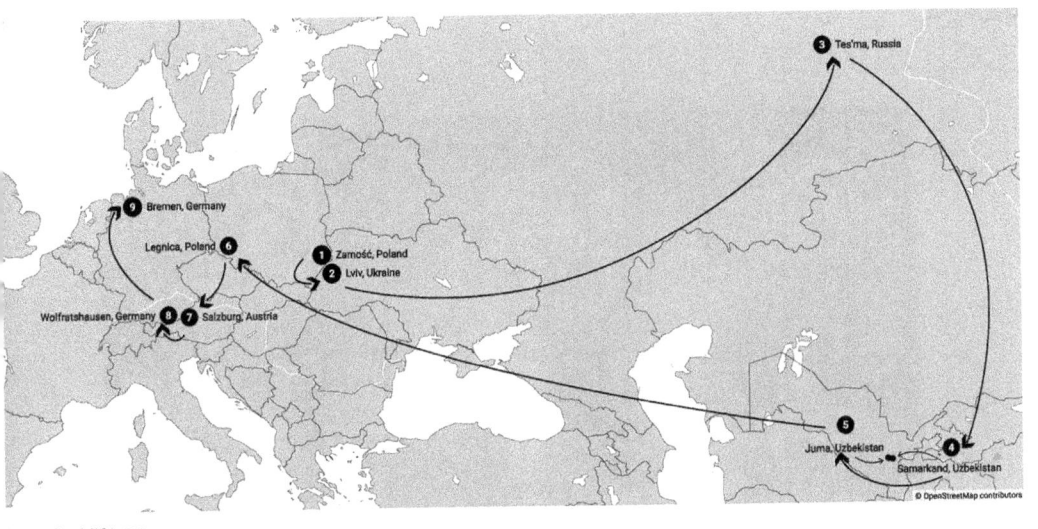

Map of the Gerson family journey, 1939-1950

204   *Lies That Matter*

A theater production of Peshka Gerzon's class in Zamość, Poland.

Mottel Gerzon with friends posing 1930s, Zamość, Poland.

Mottel Gerzon at work at the DP camp.

Lies That Matter 207

Family in Foehrenwald DP Camp, 1930s.

208   *Lies That Matter*

Gerson family names, birthdates, and false identity Blumstein names and birthdates.

Lies That Matter   209

Allan Gerzon, Foehrenwald DP Camp.

Allan in class in Foehrenwald DP Camp, 1950.

Allan, Paula and Sam Gerzon in Foehrenwald DP Camp.

Paula Gerson's International Refugee Organization DP Professional Testing Board Certificate as Rachela Blumstein, Master Dressmaker, October 1948.

Sam and Allan Gerson, Charlie and Sam Cooperman in the Bronx, NY.

> I, Mordechai Gerzon also known as Moszek Blumstein residing at 2965 Marion Avenue, Bronx, N.Y. hereby retain Saul Kies Esq., of 11 West 42nd Street, New York City as my attorney in connection with the handling of the immigration matter of myself and my wife Pola. Inconsideration of his services I agree to pay him the sum of $1000.00 payable as follows: the sum of $500.00 upon the signing of this retainer, and the balance of $500.00 upon the naturalization of myself and my wife as U.S.citizens or upon our obtaining legal residence in this country, whichever is earliest.
>
> December 11, 1957

Morton Gerson contract with immigration lawyer to gain formal citizenship, Dec 1957.

Morton and Paula Gerson's US Certificates of Naturalization, April 1958.

Zamość survivors at unveiling of cemetery site.

216 *Lies That Matter*

Allan Gerson speaking on a panel.

Lies That Matter 217

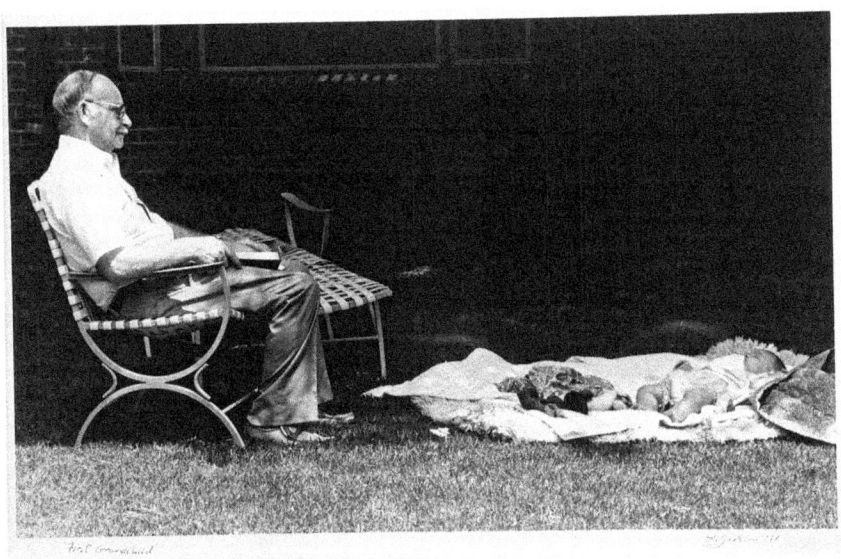

Photograph by Allan Gerson of his father watching his first grandchild, 1978.

Morton and Paula Gerson, photographed by Allan Gerson.

Allan Gerson's photograph of his mother Paula Gerson and aunt Raya Eskin in front of Zamość Memorial, 1991.

Lies That Matter 219

Allan Gerson at Zamość Memorial, pointing to "We Shall Never Forget," circa 2009.

Merissa Nathan Gerson at her grandparent's synagogue in Zamosc, Poland in 2011 after installing a new mezuzah and marking the next generation.

Sam Gerson, Allan Gerson, and Sol Cooperman in 2018.

Allan Gerson and Joan Nathan honored at the 2017 *Moment Magazine* gala.

About the Author

ALLAN GERSON, a maverick international lawyer, was widely recognized as the first American attorney to successfully sue a foreign government for complicity in acts of terrorism. He chronicled his groundbreaking work in "The Price of Terror: How the Families of the Victims of Pan Am 103 Brought Libya to Justice" (with Jerry Adler). Among Dr. Gerson's other books is "The Kirkpatrick Mission: Diplomacy Without Apology," documenting his years as senior counsel to the U.S. ambassador to the United Nations. He also was a trial attorney at the U.S. Department of Justice, a senior fellow at the American Enterprise Institute and Council on Foreign Relations, and a distinguished professor of international law at George Mason University. Dr. Gerson earned a J.D. from New York University Law School (1969), an LL.M. from the Hebrew University of Jerusalem (1972), and a J.S.D. from Yale Law School (1976). He was married to the cookbook author Joan Nathan, and was the father of their three children. Dr. Gerson died December 1, 2019.

www.ingramcontent.com/pod-product-compliance
Lightning Source LLC
Chambersburg PA
CBHW051047160426
43193CB00010B/1093